THE ONE GOAL

MASTER THE ART OF GOAL SETTING, WIN
YOUR INNER BATTLES, AND ACHIEVE
EXCEPTIONAL RESULTS

THIBAUT MEURISSE

CONTENTS

INTRODUCTION

 Give me a stock clerk with a goal, and I will give you a man who will make history. Give me a man without a goal, and I will give you a stock clerk.

— J.C. PENNY

Which scenario applies to you? The stock clerk or the person without a goal?

Sadly, most people spend more time writing their grocery lists than they will writing down their life goals. Unfortunately, this is true for about 95% of the population. Most people put more time into figuring out what they'd like for dinner than trying to answer some of life's most important questions. These crucial queries can be summed up in the following list:

- How can I obtain my dream career?
- What must I do to wake up excited and ready to get things done?
- How can I create an amazing relationship with my partner?

What must I do to experience more love and deeper connections?

- How can I create financial freedom so I can express my creativity and spend time on things that truly matter to me?
- How can I experience more happiness and contentment in my life?
- How can I live life such that I'm free of deathbed regrets?

Are you asking yourself these kinds of questions on a regular basis? I hope this book provides an opportunity for you to rethink your life, discover what really matters to you, and take action on your goals.

Who is this guide for?

This guide is designed for people who are truly committed to making drastic life changes. These people are determined to design the life they know they deserve. When applied on a daily basis, the information in this book will yield massive changes in multiple areas of your life.

It's important to note, however, that the intensity of these changes is up to you. It depends on how committed you are to taking action on the information you're presented with. I hope you'll use this book as a blueprint for every goal you set and revisit it as needed. In fact, I highly encourage you to read this book as often as necessary to master the concepts introduced in it.

I'll do whatever I can to support you throughout this book. To this end, I've included a free workbook and a series of ten videos made just for you. If you have any questions, don't hesitate to contact me at: thibaut.meurisse@gmail.com and I'll get back to you as soon as I can.

I understand that achieving exciting goals and creating a great life takes a significant amount of time and effort. I know how easy it is to get off track. We're in the same boat here! I encourage you to check out my blog and follow me on YouTube, as this will help you stick to your goals in the long run. I use both platforms to share extra tips on goals and personal development. I'm on a journey towards my goals as well, so I'm looking forward to seeing us grow in the coming years. Remember that the path to your goals is a marathon, not a sprint.

If you're unfamiliar with goal-setting, I suggest starting with my book *Goal Setting: The Ultimate Guide to Set Goals That Truly Excite You.* It serves as a good introduction to goal-setting and includes many practical tips. Feel free to check out the testimonial of a reader named Mark at the following link:

http://whatispersonaldevelopment.org/testimonial.

Additionally, you might want to check out my author page:

http://amazon.com/author/thibautmeurisse

WHAT YOU'LL LEARN FROM THIS BOOK

What you'll learn from this book

This book will cover the following 8 topics:

1. Setting truly meaningful goals that will have a tangible impact on your life
2. Getting crystal clear on your "why" and becoming genuinely excited about your goals (so much so that you can't wait to work on them!)
3. Setting your goals with optimal effectiveness
4. Developing a mastery mindset that will help you get results with future goals
5. Turbocharging your ability to persevere through challenges
6. Consistently tracking your goals for optimal results
7. Implementing powerful daily habits to support your goals
8. Redesigning your environment to better support your goals

Take Action

Throughout this book, we'll be talking heavily about the importance of an exceptional mindset. The ability to take action on what you learn is one of the critical components of an extraordinary mindset. You don't want to be an information junkie who can't use the knowledge they gain. The fact that you purchased this book tells me you want results. You want a serious return on your investment. And you'll get just that, provided you maintain your commitment.

I've included concrete calls to action at various points in the book to encourage you to use what you learn. I'm a recovering information junkie myself, so I know how hard it can be to stop consuming and start doing. That's why I created a detailed workbook to be used in tandem with this book. The workbook is intended to help you take consistent action each day.

YOUR FREE BONUS

Make sure you download the workbook and the free bonuses by typing the following URL in your browser:

http://whatispersonaldevelopment.org/the-one-goal

When you download the workbook, you'll also receive plenty of other resources including:

- Two Free eBooks (The 5 Commandments of Personal Development, How to Triple Your Productivity Within A Month)
- A series of 10 videos to further help you with your goal
- A playlist of some of the best videos around goal setting

These resources will assist you in the journey towards your goals. They'll also help you take action on your newfound knowledge.

Most problems can be solved by taking action, which is why mediocre results typically stem from insufficient action. To avoid this, I strongly suggest you fully commit yourself to doing whatever it takes to achieve your goals. I'll be doing this right along with you. Like I said before, we're in the same boat, and I'll do everything I can to support you in your journey.

If you have any difficulties downloading the workbook make sure you contact me at thibaut.meurisse@gmail.com

I've also included the workbook at the end of this book. Feel free to use it.

Now, let's get started!

1

ASSESSING YOUR GOAL-SETTING SKILLS

How good of a goal-setter are you?

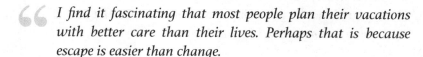 *I find it fascinating that most people plan their vacations with better care than their lives. Perhaps that is because escape is easier than change.*

— JIM JOHN

Before we start working on your goals, I'd like you to take a simple survey that will give you an idea of how good your goal-setting skills are. Goal-setting sounds simple on paper, but, as with many things, it's not something they teach us in school. It's often more complicated than it looks. Now for the survey:

Goal Setting Skills Assessment

1. Do you have a list of written goals? If so, how often do you look at it?

2. How often do you set goals? (Daily, weekly, or just for New Year's resolutions?)
3. How often have you achieved the outcomes you desire?
4. Do you have a clear, written plan describing how you'll achieve your goals?
5. Do you have a system that keeps you accountable? (An accountability partner or coach, for example.)
6. How often do you think of your goals?
7. How often do you break promises to others? By this I mean saying "yes" to something but failing to do it, or promising something you know you won't do.
8. How frequently do you break your promises to yourself? By this I mean promising yourself you'll do something but never getting around to it, or promising things you know you won't deliver on.
9. Do you visualize your goals on a regular basis?
10. Do you share your goals with others?
11. Do you reward yourself for the progress you make?
12. How accurate is the following statement: *I know a lot, but don't apply it to my life as much as I should.*

Now that you've completed this survey, you've got a better idea of where you stand. We're going to work on improving the areas in which you're falling behind. You won't just learn to become a good goal-setter, you'll learn to become a *great* one!

~

Actions step

Answer the survey questions in your workbook (section I. Assessing Your Goal-Setting Skills)

~

You'll find a detailed explanation for each question in the section "Goal Setting Skills Assessment - Survey Explanations" at the end of this book. These explanations can also be found in the workbook.

SETTING GENUINELY EXCITING GOALS

What do you want?

 Some people die at 25 and aren't buried until 75.

— BENJAMIN FRANKLIN

This question may sound simple, but it's safe to say that few people stop to properly answer it. It's easy to spend energy trying to solve the wrong problem, which is why so many people and companies hire coaches and consultants. Is it possible that you're making the same mistake? If you don't know your core values and what you want in life, you can spend years chasing the wrong goals. This will become particularly obvious when you achieve your goal only to find it unfulfilling.

People tend to fall into one of these two traps:

- Possessing goals and dreams but refusing to pursue them due to fear, social pressure, or limiting beliefs

- Being utterly unaware of what they want in life

You don't want to do either of these things, so I'd like you to answer the following question: What do you truly want in your life?

Personally, I believe we all have things we enjoy and are good at. These are things we could become excellent at if we put enough focus and energy into them.

You might feel you're bad at most things in life. That, however, doesn't matter because almost anything can be learned. You can become proficient in anything you set your mind to, as long as you give it enough time and energy. You'll also need to approach it with the right mindset. If you do those two things, there's nothing you can't master!

Bear in mind that you don't have to be great at everything to create an amazing life. You don't need to be a jack-of-all-trades. In fact, mastering just two or three skills is one of the most effective ways to build self-confidence. As you gain expertise, you'll learn to replicate your success in other areas of your life.

Taking the time to set goals that reflect what's most important to you will help you find your calling. It will also ensure you spend each day working on something meaningful. Now, I'd like to ask you one more time: What Do You Want?

Each word in this question has a powerful meaning. Let's give each one a more detailed look.

WHAT

What exactly do you want? How can you be more specific about it? The word "what" asks you to discover the "why" behind your goal. You must figure out the emotional benefits you're searching for. Are you looking for a sense of purpose? Do you want security, long for freedom, or crave recognition?

YOU

What do *you* want? It might sound obvious, but "you" means, well, YOU. This word asks what you want, not what friends, family, society, or any other outside influences want. Ignore their expectations and focus on what you, and *only* you, want deep down inside.

Here's an excellent question to ask yourself:

If I had no friends, family, or social pressures, what would I do with my life? Take some time to let that question sink in.

REALLY

Well, what do you *really* want? What is it you want yet talk yourself out of because it's "unrealistic"? There's got to be something!

Ask yourself this: If I were guaranteed to succeed at everything I do, what would I like to achieve?

WANT

What do you really *want*? What is it that genuinely excites you? The word "want" is synonymous with words like desire, longing, and craving. So what are you eager to make happen?

Let me ask once more, what do you really want? Don't limit yourself! Just imagine being able to have anything you want in life. And I mean *anything*. What would it be?

~

Action step

Use your workbook to record all your goals. Spend as much time as you need on this. Write down every goal, idea, and dream that comes to mind (section II. Clarifying your goals – 1. Getting crystal clear)

Selecting your ONE goal

Ask yourself the following question, which comes courtesy of Brian Tracy: If a genie said you could achieve one (and ONLY one) of your goals in the next 24 hours, which one would it be? Circle it once you've made your decision.

There we go! This is the goal we're going to focus on throughout this book. Focusing on your ONE goal will make it much easier to apply the mindset and strategies we'll cover. Once you learn to apply the knowledge herein to that specific goal, you'll be able to replicate the process for every other goal you have.

Make sure you select a goal you want to focus on for the next few months. In doing so, you'll be able to practice what you learn and get the most out of this book.

~

Action step

Write your ONE goal in the workbook (section II. Clarifying your goals – 2. Selecting your ONE goal)

~

The power of written goals

At this point, I'd like you to write down your ONE goal on a piece of paper.

Writing your goal down is a powerful way to start your journey towards it. There are two mains reason for this.

First off, **it tells your mind that you're serious about your goals.** Your ONE goal is no longer a vague idea in your head, it's now written on paper. When you make an important decision, such as getting married or buying a house, what do you do? You sign written documents. When written down, your ONE goal goes from invisible to tangible.

Secondly, recording your goals **forces you to clarify them.** It's virtually impossible to write down something you aren't clear on, so getting your goals on paper is a great way to ensure you fully understand them.

Write down the ONE goal you circled above. Don't worry about finding the perfect goal. You can always revise it later on.

Breaking down your goal

The goal you've chosen may be something long-term that will take a few years to achieve. Don't let that worry you though, because we're going to chunk it down into manageable tasks you can start working on today! No matter how big a goal is, it's just a succession of numerous, small steps taken each day.

If your goal is long-term (as in something that will take more than a year to achieve) break it down into a yearly goal. What exactly could you achieve in a year that would move you closer to your long-term goal? Remember to use the SMART method mentioned below.

SMART stands for:

- **Specific:** What exactly do you want? What are you trying to achieve?
- **Measurable:** Can you easily assess your progress? How will you know you've reached your goal?
- **Achievable:** Is it achievable? Is the timeframe realistic? Can you put in the required effort despite your other responsibilities?
- **Relevant:** Is the goal aligned with your values? Does it excite you?
- **Time-bound:** Do you have a clear deadline for your goal?

Action step

Use the workbook to cut your goal into yearly, quarterly, and monthly goals. See section II. Clarifying your goals – 3. Chunking down your goal. Feel free to use a blank sheet of paper to brainstorm and reverse engineer the short-term actions from your long-term goal.

~

What is your why?

 When the why gets stronger, the how gets easier.

— JIM ROHN

Most big dreams are brutally murdered solely because they seem out of reach or beyond the realm of possibility. Perhaps these dreams are genuinely out of reach, but you won't know if you don't try. Unfortunately, most of us ignore what we really want in favor of something more "realistic", and then we wonder why we feel unfulfilled and discontent.

Motivation and enthusiasm come only to those who pursue their true calling and go after what they genuinely want. It will elude you so long as you settle for what's "realistic". Think of it this way: Reaching for the stars and landing on the moon is far better than fulfilling a lackluster goal that doesn't truly fulfill you. As Jim Rohn said: Don't set your goals too low. If you don't need much, you won't become much.

A common mistake most people make is focusing excessively on the "how". They think their goal is unrealistic simply because they don't (yet) know how to achieve it. This uncertainty then drives them to choose a more realistic one. This is precisely why I asked you to forget all limitations in our previous exercise.

You have to understand that a goal is something that exists to stretch your limits. It's designed to help you reach the stars. If you already had everything necessary to achieve your goals, you probably would have reached them by now, right? If not, you'd find them pretty easy to accomplish. There would be absolutely no challenge involved. And where's the fun in that?

The true value of a goal lies entirely in the person you must become to achieve it. Your goal will require learning new skills, increasing your perseverance, strengthening your discipline, or improving your confidence. On many occasions, it will push you beyond your comfort zone. After all, if you keep doing the same thing you've always done, you'll keep getting the same results!

Creating a business has been one of the best challenges in my personal development journey thus far. Before pursuing this goal, I lacked persistence and tended to give up easily. It has forced me to become more resilient. As a result, I'm now significantly more confident in my ability to achieve my goals. I'll continually stretch myself going forward to achieve the results I desire.

You don't need to worry about the "how" of your goal yet. What you need to do is to focus on your "why". As your "why" becomes stronger, the "how" will start unfolding.

Remember that your "why" will always be more powerful than anything else. Create a "why" that strongly resonates with you, as that's what will provide the necessary drive to achieve your goal.

What is the "why" behind your ONE goal?

Now that you have your ONE goal, it's time to figure out the details of the "why" behind it.

People often end up pursuing the wrong goals and are sorely disappointed when the happiness they expect upon achieving the goal doesn't come. Even with the right goals, you have to remember that it's rarely the goal in itself that you desire. You're after the emotional benefits you hope to receive from achieving that goal. For this reason, many people are taken by surprised when they achieve their goal only to realize it's not as fulfilling as they thought it would be.

I spent months living in the future because I hated my job and wanted so badly to be somewhere else. This, of course, created a lot of suffering. It was largely based on the belief mentioned above: One day I'll achieve my goals and live blissfully ever after.

I certainly don't encourage staying at a job that you aren't enjoying. In fact, I would urge you to do quite the opposite. That said, I believe that expecting to be happy in the future once you achieved your goals is counterproductive at best, and dangerous at worst.

It's important to enjoy the journey towards your goal. It should be fun and exciting. Your goal may take you years of work before you can actually achieve it. Do you want to struggle the entire time, or do you want to enjoy the process?

Choosing to focus on the journey rather than the goal itself is your best bet, and I will delve more deeply into why this is the case at a later point in the book. As personal development blogger Steve Pavlina so aptly states, your goals should improve your current reality. They should also be sources of enjoyment most of the time . If this isn't the case, you are almost certainly pursuing the wrong goal. You might as well drop it and search for something else that meets these criteria.

Of course, I would be lying if I told you that working on your goal is going to be a constant source of excitement. There are days when it will be tough, and you'll have to use every ounce of your willpower to move forward. If your vision is compelling enough, however, you'll be pulled towards your goal.

Look at your ONE goal now.

- Why does this goal even matter to you?
- What specifically are you trying to achieve?
- How do you expect your goal to make you feel?

In the following section, we'll spend more time ensuring you focus on the right goal. We'll do this by taking a deeper look at your core values and figuring out what genuinely matters to you.

~

Action step

Write down why your goal matters to you (section II. Clarifying your goals – 4. Clarifying your why)

~

What emotional benefits do you seek?

We all have certain core values, such as security, freedom, family, integrity, or passion. Before you start working on your goal, it's important to identify your personal values and align your goal with them. If you don't, you'll lose motivation and feel empty upon achieving your goal.

You'll find list of core values online. Simply do a Google search for "list of core values". I encourage you to take time to identify which values resonate most with you. Below is a list of the core values that matter most to me. For more details, feel free to refer the article "Identify Your Core Values" on my blog.

- **Freedom:** I'm free to travel and hold a job I desire without other people telling me what to do.
- **Passion:** I have passion for what I do, and I follow it in my everyday life, regardless of the challenges I may face.
- **Truth:** I'm constantly looking for the truth, as no real

progress can be made without it. Awareness is the prerequisite to change.

- **Integrity:** I refuse to do what I feel is wrong, even when everyone else is doing it. I'm willing to sacrifice a lot to stay true to my ethics.
- **Courage:** I'm facing my fears so that I can improve myself, unleash my full potential, and become the real me.
- **Health:** I want to be healthy and have more energy. I want to live longer and accomplish many things.
- **Selflessness:** I help those around me regardless of whether they're my friend or how much they do or don't like me.
- **Fairness:** I try my best to be fair to people and avoid giving special treatment to family and friends.
- **Growth:** I take joy in working on myself and learning new skills. As a result, I want to encourage others to do the same.
- **Uniqueness:** I believe I'm unique and shouldn't be afraid of standing out and doing things that genuinely matter to me.

In the words of Jim Carrey: "I hope everybody could get rich and famous and will have everything they ever dreamed of, so they will know that it's not the answer." Understanding your core values will help you make better decisions in your life. It will also keep you from wasting time on the wrong goals. Each time you come up with new goals, you'll be able to assess their worthiness by analyzing how well they match with your core values.

If, for instance, freedom is one of your core values, will you take a job that requires spending sixty to seventy hours a week in an office? The salary may be attractive, but you'll be miserable if this job is not in line with your core values.

If you value integrity and honesty, will you take a job that requires you to lie or deceive people on a daily basis?

If you're a passionate person, will you choose a job that requires just 35 hours of work per week but bores you to death, or one that requires a 70-hour workweek but that you're madly in love with?

Knowing your core values is crucial to designing a life and career you truly enjoy. If your life is out of sync with who you fundamentally are, you'll feel a painful disconnect.

You don't have to compare yourself to your friends. Some of them may enjoy a stable 9 to 5 job that they consider to be just "okay", while you want to put your heart and your soul into what you love, even if it's not as stable, involves longer workdays, or means earning less than they do.

Some of your friends might be working hard and making a lot of money at a job they hate. Yet you may secretly wish you could make as much money as they do. But, ask yourself this: Do I really want to work hard at something I despise just for the money? Do I want to spend most of my waking hours doing something I can't stand for the rest of my life? Does this sound like the proper way to value the precious time you've been given on this planet? Sure, making a lot of money may allow you to have a bigger house and drive a better car, but is it really worth it if you're miserable? That's a question you must answer for yourself.

If you want to avoid spending years pursuing the wrong goals, I encourage you to dig deeper and record your core values in the workbook. Don't worry about making it perfect, you'll be able to fine-tune your list over time as you learn more about yourself.

∾

Action step

Write down your core values in the workbook (section II. Clarifying Your Goals – 5. Aligning your goals with your core values)

∾

Now that you have a list of your core values, it's time to prioritize them. Again, there is no right or wrong answer here, just go with your gut. What value in your list is your top priority? Is it integrity? Is it freedom? Is it passion? Is it family?

Now look at your ONE goal: How does it fit with your core values? Does it allow you to live in a way that's in sync with them? Do you have a strong emotional connection with your goal?

The "why" behind your goal and how you connect to it emotionally will directly impact your ability to achieve it. Obviously, the stronger you feel about your goal, the more motivated and inspired you'll be. Working on it regularly and persevering in the face of adversity will become easier as a result. In the following section, we'll discuss the mindset required to achieve your goal.

3

CREATING AN EXTRAORDINARY MINDSET

> *We will act consistently with our view of who we truly are, whether that view is accurate or not.*
>
> — TONY ROBBINS

Do you believe you can achieve your goal?

∾

Action step

Before you continue reading, please refer to the corresponding section in the workbook and answer the following question (section III. "Creating an Extraordinary Mindset" - 1. Believing in Yourself):

On a scale of 0 to 10, how confident are you that you will achieve the one monthly goal that you just set in the next thirty days?

∾

Let me ask you a question: Do you really believe you can achieve your ONE goal? What about the other exciting goals you've never told anyone about?

Your ability to achieve any of your goals has more to do how much you believe in yourself than anything else. There's nothing external that can keep you from achieving them. Unfortunately, internal barriers can...and will. In the end, it's your ability to use the power of your mind and to create unshakable self-confidence that will determine whether you'll achieve your goals.

By the time we're old enough to decide what we want to do with our lives, we've already been told what we can and cannot do. Society, parents, teachers, friends, and even the media have already shaped our view of the world. They've formed our beliefs regarding what we can expect from the world and how we should fit into it.

In fact, T. Harv Ecker's book *The Millionaire Mindset* states that our parents' beliefs around money give us a financial blueprint that determines how much money we're "allowed" to make. For many of us, our school performance tells us that we'll never "make it", despite the fact that there are many successful people (Einstein, anyone?) who didn't do particularly well in school.

Society encourages us to live our lives in a certain way, and we typically accept the fate it hands us without challenging its underlying assumptions. We're all supposed to get good grades, go to college, join a company, work 40+ hours a week, and retire at 65 (if we're lucky). At the rate things are going, it won't be long before the standard retirement age rises to seventy or older.

We're supposed to go into debt in our twenties by taking on expensive student loans, and find someone to marry. After that, we're supposed to spend thousands of dollars on a wedding ring (which has more to do with jewelry companies trying to make money than actual romance). Then we're supposed to spend even more money on a wedding ceremony. We're also expected to buy a big house and drive a nice car. No wonder most of us spend 40 plus years at jobs we hate just to make ends meet.

The thing is, this is just one example of how you can live your life. It's not a blueprint that should be followed blindly. You might have another vision of what you want your life to be. Maybe you just don't care about work/life balance and love what you do so much that you want to work fifteen hours a day, seven days a week like Gary Vaynerchuk or Grant Cardone. Or perhaps you believe in work/life integration like Tony Robbins. That is, you want to work towards something with your family that you're all deeply passionate about. It may be hard work, but you're reaching for the same goal together.

You might be someone who has few material needs and wants to work just 25 hours a week while dedicating your free time to inexpensive activities like reading, writing, or running. On the other hand, you might want to take a 6-month vacation every year. Or perhaps you want to work as a freelancer so you can earn money while traveling the world. Or maybe you want to retire at 45.

I believe all of these scenarios are possible. The first step is allowing yourself to entertain the idea that what you want is actually possible. The second step is realizing the need to transform your current beliefs and match them with what you want to achieve.

What you think of as your beliefs often belong to someone else. They usually come from somewhere in your subconscious and have been heavily influenced by the people and things around you. They have little, if anything, to do with what you're actually capable of. Fortunately, they aren't set in stone. You can choose to change them until they fully support your goal. It's your call.

In reality, there are an unlimited number of actions you could take at any moment in your life. Every second that passes opens the door to millions of things you could choose to do. Reading this book is just one of the many things you could be choosing to do right now.

How many actions could you theoretically take right now if you really wanted to? How many options have you subconsciously ruled out? For instance, could you commit to making drastic changes to totally transform an area of your life that you're dissatisfied with? Is it a possibility? Could you reach a point where you're so sick of your current situation (or so passionate about a specific goal) that you make a binding decision to change your life at all costs?

Yes, you certainly could. The reason you haven't made decisions like this yet is because you might not have freed yourself from your current belief system. You might still hold disempowering beliefs that determine what you think is possible for you, what you think you should or shouldn't do, and what you think you deserve.

No matter what your goal, there is a way, or perhaps even many ways, to achieve it. Ultimately, your ability to achieve your goal depends on the beliefs you create around it. It's also heavily dependent upon your level of creativity, passion, and perseverance, among other qualities we'll mention later on.

Objective reality is a myth

 There's one earth, but billions of worlds.

— Mooji

Do you realize that no human being on this planet has experienced objective reality, and no one ever will? Right now, you and I are experiencing a different reality. That subjective reality is the result of our personal interpretations of reality via our 5 senses.

Indeed, we never experience reality directly, our brain simply decodes reality according to a certain set of rules. That's why we're unable to hear certain sounds or distinguish between certain colors. We also have no way to know how much more there is to perceive beyond what we can directly see. Surprisingly, we can't even tell whether reality exists out there or if it's all in our heads. We could very well be living in the Matrix. How would we know?

However, our interpretation of reality doesn't stop with our five senses. We are also interpreting the world through our thoughts, which creates our own "subjective world".

Does your subjective world support your goals?

Because there is no objective reality, there's no real barrier in the outside world that could stop you from reaching your goals. The only real barriers are mental ones. As such, most of your goals (even the really crazy ones!) are actually possible. Easily achievable? Probably not. But possible? YES! Just look at all the people in the history of the word who have achieved incredible things that were once considered impossible.

There is, for instance, no objective reality that prevents us from going to the moon. Yet if our subjective reality didn't allow us as humans to be crazy enough to entertain the idea, we would never have accomplish that feat, which was once completely unrealistic.

Nobody believed that a mile could be run in less than 4 minutes before 1954, when Roger Bannister did in 3 minutes and 59 seconds. Shortly after that, many athletes were suddenly able to run a mile in less than four minutes. What changed? Their beliefs changed. Seeing someone run a mile that was shattered their subjective world and broke their mental barriers. They had proof that it was possible, and that changed everything.

In the same vein, you must redesign your subjective world by shifting your beliefs. You have to do it such that you'll start manifesting the desired behaviors and actions you need to achieve your goals. To do that, you must fully align your beliefs and thoughts with what you want make happen.

If you don't genuinely believe in your goals, you'll begin sabotaging your efforts on a subconscious level. Fortunately, you have the power within you to reprogram your mind and change your beliefs, thus creating a brand new subjective world that will fully support your goals.

Believe it until you become it: creating a goal-oriented identity

To make your goal a reality, you must create a new identity that is congruent with that goal. The objective is to become the type of person who has, or will, achieve that goal.

For instance, when I started writing books and articles on personal development, I didn't see myself as a writer. In a typical conversation, I described myself as someone who "has a blog and writes personal development articles." I would refer to my books as "very short", "very simple", and "not a big deal". What legitimate writer would say things like that?

At some point I realized that, if I wanted to make a career out of writing, I'd have to redefine how I perceived myself and change how I conveyed my passion. I would have to take it more seriously. That's when I started changing the words I used to describe my blogging and writing activities. I wasn't "just" a blogger anymore. I wasn't writing simple books that weren't a big deal. I was creating an online business. I was an entrepreneur. I was a writer. I was the author of several books published on Amazon. I was really making a difference in people's lives.

These days I introduce myself as someone who's building an online business. I tell people that I'm a writer. Changing what I say and finding a new way to discuss myself and my work has transformed the whole way I perceive my goals. It impacts how I think and compels me to act and behave differently.

It's essential that you, too, work on creating an identity related to your goal that you firmly believe in. As you create a new identity and broadcast it to the world, you'll start acting in a way that's more and more congruent with that identity. It then impacts the way you interact with other people.

For example, introducing myself as a writer makes it easier to network with other writers. I also feel more motivated to improve my writing skills, create better content, improve the formatting of my books, finding better designs for my book covers, and join writers groups. I'm a writer, after all, and it is what any decent writer does!

The more I introduce myself and my work with confidence, the more I tell my subconscious mind that I'm actually a writer, and the more I start to believe it. This concept applies to all of us.

Let me give you another example. Let's say your goal is to lose weight. Rather than focusing on weight loss, you can start thinking of yourself as a healthy person. It's just who you are, you're a healthy person. You can see yourself as a person who enjoys walking and exercising, a person who takes care of their body.

When you interact with other people, you can start talking about yourself as someone who takes care of their health. If you're currently overweight, you can mention that you're taking small daily steps to become healthier.

Your goal-oriented identity is how you would introduce yourself and your goal to someone you've just met. It goes beyond a simple mental exercise. I recommend writing down precisely how you would introduce yourself and your goals to a stranger, then practice it every day in front of a mirror. See it as an elevator pitch you would give to someone you've just met. You can also practice visualizing yourself talking about your goal or vision with confidence. Make that vision as specific as possible.

Example: Let's say I want to introduce myself as a writer. Here's are some of the things I could say:

I'm a writer. I've successfully published personal development books that have been read by people around the world. I've helped thousands of people achieve their goals, and I regularly receive thank you emails from readers regarding how much they loved my books and the impact my work has had on their lives. Some of my readers loved my first book so much that they recommended it to family and friends.

What about you? What new identity will you create to achieve your goal?

Complete the following sentence:

I am_____

∽

Action step

To create your goal-oriented identity, refer to the section "Creating your goal identity" in the workbook.

(section III. "Creating an Extraordinary Mindset" - 2. Creating your goal-related identity)

∽

Holding the right assumptions about success

If your basic assumptions are wrong, your actions will be flawed and you'll fail to get tangible results. Unfortunately, most of us have the wrong assumptions about what it really takes to achieve our goals. Marketers want us to believe that we can get rich quickly or lose weight easily. As a result, many of us have developed a short-term mentality that dictates our day-to-day actions. We think we can take a "magic pill" that will solve all our problems. This leads to several consequences you may be familiar with:

- Believing things should be easy and fast to the point that we give up when we don't see any results
- When we don't see results quickly enough, we jump from one program to another enticed by the exceptional results we're promised

This is all based upon the dangerous assumption that we "deserve" results and can get them without much effort. The fact is, reality doesn't care whether or not you deserve to achieve your goal. Do what it takes and you'll get results, rely on the magic pill and you won't. Period.

You must be brutally honest with yourself and uncover the real reasons you've failed to get results in the past. If you don't, change will be impossible. Did you give up too easily? Were you overly optimistic? Did you fail to assess the difficulty of the challenges that lay ahead of you? Did you lack belief in yourself and your goals?

Now, I'd like you to spend some time to think about the reasons you failed to get the results you wanted in the past. This is an important part of the goal-setting process.

∼

Action step

Spend a few minutes answering the questions below using the workbook (section III. – 3. Aligning yourself with reality and facing the truth)

- What is one goal that you wanted to achieve in the past but didn't?
- According to you, what are the reasons why you failed to achieve that goal?
- What could have you done differently to help you achieve that goal?

∼

Mastering the art of perseverance

> *In the long run, people usually do achieve their goals if they persist, stay flexible, and don't give up. The biggest challenge for most people is persisting long enough to win the mental game.*

Most people say they tried, but did they? In most cases, they didn't even get started. They tried for a few months before giving up. Or, in the case of a huge goal, they tried for a couple of years before giving up. Is that really trying? If there's something you seriously want to do, wouldn't it make sense to commit to working on it for a long stretch of time? There are some goals that could take years, or perhaps even a lifetime, to complete, so shouldn't you be ready to work on your goal for several years?

Unfortunately, lack of perseverance is one of the main reasons most people waste their potential and fail to achieve their most important goals. Developing perseverance will yield exceptional results in your life. It's what will allow you to experience breakthroughs after plateauing for weeks or even months.

Keep in mind that perseverance is a skill, and as with any other skill, it can be learned and honed through mental preparation. In this section, we'll discuss how you can dramatically increase your level of perseverance while working towards your goal.

Mentally preparing yourself

Most people fail to achieve their goal because their initial assumptions are wrong. They see the road ahead as a highway that will take them straight to their goal, but it's actually a bumpy road full of nasty surprises and obstacles. They start their journey with a Sedan when what they need is a 4X4 and, sure enough, they stop halfway through.

Your ability to understand what the journey to your goal consists of is a crucial step towards achieving it. It's essential to mentally prepare yourself for all the obstacles you'll face along the way.

The truth is, many things can, and will, go wrong. What you thought would take you 6 months may take you two years. That brilliant idea you thought everybody would love might go totally ignored. You may be stumbling in the dark for months before seeing results from the business you're working on. You'll feel like giving up many times. I certainly did. And I would be lying if I said there weren't times when I felt high levels of self-doubt. In fact, I'd often wonder if all the time and energy spent writing books and blogging was actually worth it.

However, I'd like you to remember that none of these challenges are signs you should give up. They're merely signs that you're on a journey towards your goal and that you must keep going. After all, speedbumps and roadblocks are just standard parts of the process.

Life will always eliminate people who aren't committed enough to their goal, and that's how it should be. Understanding that obstacles are perfectly normal will go a long way in helping you achieve the goals that matter to you. I'd like you to use the following two words as your mantras for the coming months and years: **patience** and **perseverance**. These two qualities alone will take your results to a whole new level. Be more patient! Be more perseverant!

With the right amounts of patience and perseverance, you can overcome almost any obstacle, even when the odds are all against you. On the other hand, talent itself won't lead to exceptional results. In fact, it's not uncommon to see average people who, having developed great resilience over time, outshine even the most talented people in their field.

Now, let's see what you can do to mentally prepare yourself and ensure that you become more perseverant while pursuing your goal.

To start, think of everything that can go wrong and write down what you'll do if these things do happen. Make sure you imagine the most extreme cases you can think of. Doing so will ensure that you aren't taken by surprise when things go wrong, and it will help you build greater resilience.

Next, decide what would make you give up on your goal. "I'll do whatever it takes" is not enough. What does "whatever it takes" mean? The more you can envision what could go wrong, the better you'll be able to face adversities as they manifest along the way. If nothing would make you give up, that's fantastic. Still, make sure you envision what the worst case scenario would look like.

What's the worst that could happen? We tend to be overly optimistic, so make sure you envision the worst.

Example:

- My website has been hacked and I lost all my articles, my list of subscribers, and my income. I have to start from scratch. Can I handle that?
- Despite working on my business day in and day out for 3 years, I've actually lost money. Can I handle that? (True story)
- I've lost all my data and have to write two books from scratch. Can I do it? (Another true story)
- I've been on a diet for more than two months but I've hardly lost any weight. Can I keep going?

Action step

Spend a few minutes answering the questions below using the workbook (section III. – 4. Mastering the art of extreme perseverance)

- What would be your worse cases scenarios? Write them down.
- What would make you give up on your goals?

Examples:

- If I made absolutely no money after a year working on my online business
- If I didn't sell at least X copies of my book within 6 months

I assume that your current goal is something you're sincerely excited about. As such, you shouldn't give up too easily. During the first few months, many people are excited to work on their new goals. Yet when they fail to get results after six months or a year, they just quit. This sort of mindset will never allow you to achieve exceptional results in your life.

If your goal is something you really care about, why would you give up after one year? It's much wiser to hang in there for at LEAST a few years before you even *consider* giving up. Remember that success takes time and you must be both patient and perseverant.

Developing a healthy relationship with "failure"

> *No man ever achieved worthwhile success who did not, at one time or another, find himself with at least one foot hanging well over the brink of failure.*
>
> — NAPOLEON HILL

Your brain can achieve incredible things, but it can't play its part unless you play yours. That is, you need to provide your brain with regular feedback so it can learn and grow. This feedback is what people generally call "failure". Without it, you'll never learn enough to get where you want to go.

Many people will never achieve their goals thanks to fear of failure. In fact, many of them won't even take the first step towards their dreams. On the other hand, truly successful people are willing to fail again and again and, because they fail more than anybody else, they eventually figure things out.

During the process that we call success, you'll inevitably encounter bumps in the road, you may have to make a detour or to do a U-turn.

You may have to slow down. As long as you keep driving, however, you're likely to reach your destination.

Reframing failure

Failure isn't a big deal in and of itself. It's the meaning you give to it that wreaks havoc, effects your emotions, and leads to giving up on your goal. Having lots of "failures" in your life doesn't mean anything. It's not like you can reach a point where you fail so much that you can't succeed anymore. That's not how it works. If anything, it's usually quite the opposite.

As Tony Robbins says, "The past doesn't equal the future." Repeated failure in the past is by no means an indicator of your future. It is often an indicator that you must change your beliefs and do things differently going forward.

Another point that people don't fully grasp is that failure and success are one. Contrary to popular belief, failure and success aren't separate entities, with failure on one side and success on the other. Failure and success are part of the same process that you must follow to achieve your goal.

Indeed, you cannot have success without facing temporary setbacks and disappointments along the way. That's because you need "failures" to let you know that what you're currently doing isn't working. Failures are the feedback you need so that you can get back on track and achieve your long-term goals.

Hence, taking the time to learn as much as you can from your failures is a crucial part of achieving your goal. Later on, we'll have an in-depth discussion regarding the importance of focusing on the process we call "success".

Learning to be patient

Are you a passionate person? Do you regularly pull all-nighters, or work 80-plus hours a week? If so, that's great. There's nothing wrong with working hard. However, you must also remember that the journey is a marathon, not a sprint. Can you sustain that pace for the next three years? Five years? Ten years? Can you focus on your primary goal for an extensive period of time without being distracted or moving on to one that seems more exciting? Can you persevere for years even when you aren't getting the results you want?

Most people suffer from an extreme lack of patience. They say they want to make a living from their passion and live life on their own terms, but they give up after six months or a year. How do I know that? Well, I have to admit that I almost gave up on blogging after a year, although I made a comeback after a very long "break".

Online marketer Gary Vaynerchuk has a fantastic video in which he talks about patience. If you're curious about it, search "Gary Vaynerchuck Overnight Success" on YouTube. Here's what he has to say:

"When you email me, that you've started things, that you have the audacity to want it to be the rest of your life, the audacity, really, the entitlement that you think that you should be able to do something that you love so much for the rest of your life, that makes you enough money to be able to do it for the rest of your life, that you are giving up after four months! That you are giving up after two years! As a matter of fact, every person watching this video should be trying for that moment for the rest of their life. Period!"

Patience is one of your greatest assets, and it's highly underrated. Start seeing yourself as someone with great patience, and remind yourself on a daily basis that you do have time, and that you are in it for the long-haul.

∽

Action step

Reread this section whenever necessary, put Post-its on your desktop with

"I'm very patient" or "I love being patient" written on them, or repeat affirmations. Just keep experimenting and do whatever works for you.

~

Creating a bullet-proof timeframe

In this section, I'd like to introduce you to the concept of bullet-proof timeframe, something I've developed and successfully implemented in my personal life.

I believe there are three main reasons people fail to achieve their goals:

1. Lack of belief
2. Lack of patience
3. Lack of consistency

The bullet-proof timeframe addresses the first issues regarding patience. Lack of patience plays a huge role in giving up on your goal too fast. As you work on your goal, it's easy to get so excited about it that you lose your sense of time. Time becomes highly distorted and you become obsessed with getting fast results. You become impatient and start believing you don't have enough time to achieve your goal. That's when you generally feel like giving up. At least, that what happened to me many times.

The bullet-proof timeframe is here to address this specific problem by reminding you that you DO have time and enticing you to keep working on your goal until you reach a specific point.

The bullet-proof timeframe provides the following benefits:

- **It forces you to select a goal that truly matters to you.** Why would you care about some distant deadline two to three years from today if your goal isn't that important?
- **It reminds you that you have time.** It allows you to step

back, look at the big picture, and realize that you still have time. This, of course, enables you to become more perseverant.

- **It helps you avoid Shiny Object Syndrome.** This prevents you from jumping from one thing to the next because you feel you aren't getting results fast enough. This is a major trap that many people fall prey to.
- **It gives you the option of giving up.** You can give yourself total permission to give up, but ONLY once you've reached the deadline, and never before. This is the mindset you'll want to adopt: *I can always give up once I reach my deadline, so, for now, I'm going to hang on and keep going.*

In a project that examined the childhoods of experts in various fields, several parents reported using the following technique to prevent their children from quitting when they were sick or injured. They would tell their children that they could give up, but not before practicing and getting back to their previous skill level. This worked wonders. As the children got back to their previous skill level, they felt motivated to keep practicing. That's probably why they are experts in their fields today. They did NOT give up.

You may wonder how long the bullet-proof timeframe should be. For a major goal, I recommend a two to three-year timeline. It's a long enough time for you to get some tangible results. Note that it's very common for people to give up within a year. This is precisely the mistake I want you to avoid.

Now it's time to write down the bullet-proof timeframe you're committed to using in the workbook.

∿

Action step

Spend a few minutes to create your own bullet-proof timeframe using the workbook. (section III. – 5. Creating a bullet-proof timeframe)

~

Practicing self-compassion

Self-compassion is another important tool that can be used to increase your level of perseverance.

How often have you self-sabotaged your efforts by criticizing yourself for not being as consistent, disciplined, or intelligent as you'd like to be? If you're like most of us, you've probably done this a lot. But has it ever helped you achieve your goal?

Self-sabotaging behavior can cause you to give up on your goals and dreams, often under the false assumptions that you aren't good enough, smart enough, or are undeserving. Self-sabotage becomes yet another excuse to give up and go back to your comfortable, but likely unhappy, life.

One reason we tend to fall into that trap of self-criticism has to do with the way our brain works. Our brain loves efficiency above all else, and it would rather sabotage our efforts than to spend energy trying to change deeply ingrained habits. In many cases, self-criticism is nothing more than a trick of the mind. That's something you might want to keep in the back of your mind as you're working on your goal.

Many people also believe that they won't get anything done unless they're hard on themselves, but this is a huge misconception. Yes, people who practice self-compassion are, in truth, more perseverant.

Imagine how much energy you would save if you stopped criticizing yourself. Self-blame can lead to worrying constantly without making any progress. This makes it all the more tempting to give up on your goal. It certainly did for me in many occasions. There are times in my life where I spent days on end beating myself up. I always came to the conclusion that worrying wasn't helping anything and subsequently got back to work.

We're all victims of self-sabotaging behaviors, and the more we're able to identify them and understand their triggers, the better we'll be able to address them. These behaviors may manifest as mild depression, sadness, feelings of unworthiness, disappointment, and so on. More often than not, they're recurrent patterns triggered by specific events in our lives. As you become aware of these patterns and how they affect your emotions and quality of life, you'll be better able to overcome them.

~

Action step

Spend some time at the end of each week to assess your emotional state. Were you happy or sad? Were you motivated or uninspired? What were the potential triggers that led you to experience these emotions?

As you continue assessing your emotions week after week, you'll come up with powerful insights and shed light on some of your most persistent mental blocks. That new level of awareness will allow you to become more perseverant. It will also facilitate your progress towards your goal.

Finally, remember that self-compassion is not a sign of weakness, it is a sign of strength. It shows that you care about yourself and recognize that you're doing what you can at your own level.

Success is a process not an event

Whatever your goal is, its end result will always stem from a process you go through on a consistent basis. What people call luck is generally what happens to people who continually focus on the right process until they get results. It's impossible to be successful in life without going through a specific procedure that leads to success. Someone who focuses on the process of creating a company on a daily basis and becomes a multimillionaire is not, in my opinion, a lucky person.

While it may seem that someone is an overnight success, that's almost never the case. In reality, this person is simply being rewarded in public for the thousands of hours they spent working on their business in private. They went through the process and felt like giving up many times in the past, but persisted and continued taking the right actions.

I would like you to think of your goal as a journey you're embarking on that has all sorts of ups and downs. Every failure and setback you encounter along the way are just part of the process. The key is to keep moving forward and stay consistent. Do what you can with the time you have available. Most importantly, persevere until the bullet-proof timeframe expires and see what happens.

∽

Action step

Turn your result-oriented goal into process-oriented goal (section III. – 6. Focusing on the process)

∽

Learning to enjoy the process

When you're working on your goal, it's easy to become obsessed with results. I remember a time not so long ago when I was constantly worrying about the future and whether I'd make money from my business or wind up totally broke. I regularly felt like giving up when things didn't go as planned. This constant worry about the future was creating unnecessary suffering in my life to the point where I had to do something about it if I wanted to achieve my goals.

That's when I realized that I needed to refocus on the process, or, in other words, what I'm doing every day. I practiced living one day at a time and focusing on doing my best instead of worrying about the future. You probably already know that you should live one day at a time rather than worry about the future, but this book is all about mastery. We aren't interested in knowing various concepts on an intellectual level, what we want is to become living proof of these concepts and get results. I encourage you to form a habit of living one day at a time and focusing on what you can do today.

Imagine if you could work on your goals consistently every day regardless of the external results. How much more likely would you be to achieve your goals? What else can you do apart from working on your goals consistently each day and continuing to believe in yourself? Not much. The fact is, these are among the few things you can do.

Process-oriented goals vs. result-oriented goals

To put more emphasis on the process, it's important to focus on process-oriented goals rather than result-oriented goals. At the end of the day, you want to get the results you seek. However, it's a process-oriented approach that will ensure you actually take consistent action and get results.

Another perk of process-oriented goals is the absolute control you have over them. Below are some examples of process-oriented goals as opposed to results-oriented ones:

- Self-publishing your book vs. selling 10,000 copies of it
- Drinking water instead of soda each day for the next three months vs. losing eight pounds in three months
- Running 45 minutes every day for a year vs. winning a marathon after a year of practice
- Working two hours a day on your side business for the next 6 months vs. making $ 2,000 per month from it for the next six months

You have absolute control over those process-oriented goals. You can choose to drink water instead of soda, but you can't guarantee that you'll lose eight pounds. You can run for 45 minutes every day, but you can't guarantee that you'll win a marathon.

That's not to say you shouldn't have clear goals, because you certainly should. And, of course, that's what this book is about. My point, however, is that you may not always be able to achieve the results you want even if you work as hard as you possibly can. Yet as long as you keep focusing on the process consistently, you'll eventually get results. It might take twice as long as you expected, but if this goal is important to you, does it even matter?

Additional tip:

I always remind myself to stay focused on the process as I go through my daily morning ritual. I have stickers on my desk that say "Focus on the process", and "It's what you do every day that counts". I also say certainly things out loud, such as, "I always focus on the process and I make every single day count", or "If I keep doing what I can every single day, I will eventually become the best that I can be."

I encourage you to ask yourself the following question every day:

If I keep doing what I've done today, will I achieve my goals?

Taking the right actions

To help you focus on the process, I would like to introduce the concept of "**right actions**". You might fail to reach your goals in the short-term. Let's say you set a goal to add an additional $ 1,000 to your monthly income by the end of the year, but wind up making $100. Or perhaps, your original goal is losing ten pounds in two months but you lose 2 instead. In these scenarios, would you say that you failed to achieve your goals?

If so, I would argue that that isn't necessarily the case. We tend to overestimate what we can accomplish within timeframes of less than a year. On the other hand, we typically underestimate what we're capable of achieving over the course of a few years.

The point is: Did you take the right action? Did you work on your side business 30 minutes a day like you said you would? Did you stop drinking soda and walk for an hour a day like you said you'd do?

If you consistently take the right actions, you'll eventually get results in the long-term.

In the beginning, we rarely see the results we expect. We tend to be overly optimistic and usually fail to realize that progress is not linear. The process of achieving a goal is much like planting a seed: it needs to be watered daily. At first, nothing happens. After a while, however, it starts growing, sometimes at breakneck speed. Your job is to water the seed of your goal every day. To do this, you must take the right actions while remaining patient with the process. What else can you do?

Ask yourself the following question: Did I take the right action today?

Destroying the "Talent Myth"

 The only thing that I see that is distinctly different about me is: I'm not afraid to die on a treadmill. You might have more talent than me; you might be smarter than me. But if we get on a treadmill together, there's two things: you're getting off first, or I'm gonna die. It's really that simple.

— WILL SMITH

It's easy to get discouraged when you aren't seeing any progress. Others around you seem to learn faster than you do, and they're more talented than you are. What's the point of even trying? You might as well give up, right? Wrong. The issue isn't that everyone else is better than you. The issue is that you've fallen prey to misconceptions.

There is a huge myth around talent that seems to span the entire world. This is unfortunate, as it takes a huge toll on society in the form of millions of people not living up to their potential. If you buy into this myth, you'll pay a similar price.

I can't tell you how many Japanese people have told me how smart I was just because I can speak Japanese fluently. They act as if I'm some sort of genius, which totally dismisses the fact that I spent 10,000+ hours studying Japanese while they were partying, watching TV, or simply devoting their time to another skill. I have no predisposition to speaking a foreign language, and I started from nothing just like anyone else. This is more or less how the conversation goes:

Them: I wish I could speak English as well as you speak Japanese.

Me: Well, you can.

Them: No, I'm too old/No, I'm not good at learning languages/No, I've studied for years, but I still can't speak English...

Interestingly, I've yet to meet someone who says these things *and* has actually done the necessary work to achieve that goal they (supposedly) want to achieve. Now, I'm not suggesting that they're lazy or are being deliberately deceptive. More often than not, people who talk like this don't think they are talented enough to learn English. If they sincerely believe the story they're telling themselves, there is indeed no point in trying. At the end of the day, however, the story is only a belief. Sadly, that belief is holding the person back due to the way it impacts their subjective world.

Personally, I have no doubt that each and every one of these people could become fluent in English as long as they're willing to put in the work. There's very little they could say to convince me otherwise. If *they* don't believe they can, however, then, sure enough, they won't. This is one of the many ways people limit themselves by holding disempowering beliefs that don't reflect reality.

Believing in talent is disempowering because it often causes us to give up prematurely. When we buy into the story that we're untalented, we dismiss the power we have to improve ourselves. We forget that we have the ability to develop sophisticated patterns in our brains that will allow us to achieve in the future what seems impossible today. In short, we neglect the most extraordinary gift we've been given: our minds!

What if you knew that talent was highly overrated? What if you knew that through hard work, consistency, and perseverance, you can achieve almost anything you've ever dreamed of? Imagine how much more perseverant you'd become. If you couldn't use "I don't have talent" anymore, how would it change the way you think about your goals and dreams?

The importance of patterns

So much can be achieved once you learn to increase your perseverance. The incredibly successful people who seem amazingly talented are rarely as talented as you think. In reality, their success is usually linked with the fact that they've done the very thing you're admiring millions of times. They've practiced every day for years or even decades, which make them look like they have some kind of superpower.

For instance, I've always been amazed by chess players and their extraordinary memory. A quick glance is all it takes for them to remember the location of all the pieces on the board. Incredible! Or is it? Studies have shown that if you place the pieces on the board randomly, a chess player's memory is not significantly better than that of an average person who doesn't play chess. Why is that?

It's because, through repeated exposure to certain patterns, chess players have developed mental associations that allow them to identify thousands of different patterns with just one glance. As a result, they can make decisions in what seems like an instant. It's as if they have a supercomputer in place of their brain. When the pieces on the chessboard don't match anything they're familiar with, however, they suddenly lose their seemingly superhuman memory. This means that not even the world's best chess players are the superhuman and godlike geniuses we've been told they are.

Still don't believe me? Consider this: Studies have shown that higher IQs weren't linked with greater chess skill in masters and grandmasters. Further studies showed the same results for musicians and other groups of seemingly talented people. How is that possible? Well, you just can't become exceptional at something without internalizing thousands of patterns and creating intricate mental associations. It doesn't matter how smart or "talented" you may be, you can't develop that kind of mental prowess without innumerable hours of deliberate practice. Experts aren't born with supercomputers in their heads, but they do create them from scratch, piece by piece. They do this through practice and repetition, and you can, too!

Studies have shown that, as you would expect, people with higher IQs do tend to get better results. However, this is true only on a short-term basis. They may outperform less "talented" people for a few months or years. Yet, in the long run, it's usually those who work hardest and persevere most who reach the top.

Below is an excerpt from *Peak – Secrets from The New Science of Expertise* by Anders Ericsson and Robert Pool. Ericsson is a cognitive psychologist who has spent his career studying how people become world-class experts in their respective fields.

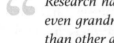 *Research has also shown that skilled adults chess players – even grandmasters – do not have systematically higher IQs than other adults with similar level of education. Nor is there any correlation between the IQs of highly skilled chess players and their chess ratings. As strange as it seems to those of us who have grown up with the tortured-but-brilliant fictional characters who excel at chess, all of the evidence says that higher intelligence is not correlated with better chess playing among adults.*

As someone who has lived in Japan for many years, I've heard about *Go* and how complex it is. There are so many combinations that the current *Go* software still can't beat its top-ranked players, as opposed to chess AI. So what about these *Go* players? You'd think they would have exceptional IQs, but that's not the case. Yet again, studies have shown that the IQs of *Go* masters weren't consistently higher than those of the general population.

Everything in life is pattern. In the end, it's your ability to recognize and internalize these patterns while creating complex, abstract associations in your mind that truly matters. Your current goal may not involve becoming a grandmaster, but it will likely require practicing and developing patterns and references that will allow you to excel at what you do. That, of course, is possible only through a mix of repetition, patience, and perseverance.

Rather than thinking others are smarter than you, realize that they're just a little bit ahead of you. That's okay, because the journey is a marathon, not a sprint. They may be a mile ahead of you, but that's not much in the scheme of things.

If you're wondering what patterns look like in different contexts, the following examples will help:

Coaching:

Even human interactions, which are rooted in psychology, contain a vast number of patterns. That's why someone who has coached thousands of people will be far better at it than someone who has only coached a few. The person with more experience will have had time to identify specific patterns and, based on these patterns, provide better results to their clients.

Sales:

In sales, customers may come up with all kind of objections, but a seasoned salesperson will be able to overcome most of them because he has faced them countless times in the past. They know what to expect because they recognize the patterns.

Logical thinking:

In order to thinking logically, we need to organize our thoughts in a certain way. As with most things, logical thinking is a pattern-based skill that can be learned. There are only so many ways you can think without straying from logic.

Art/Music:

Even creative activities such as art or music consist of patterns and are more structured than we like to admit. Picasso didn't use cubism when he first started painting. His cubism paintings were only possible because he had mastered more traditional forms of painting beforehand, which allowed him to internalize all relevant patterns before discovering new territory.

Public speaking:

Many surveys have shown that public speaking is, for many people, their greatest fear. Fortunately, it's also a learnable skill that is determined by certain patterns. The more you practice, the better you'll become at using eye contact and employing different vocal tones. Your body language will become more convincing as well. You'll also get better at using emotions, humor, and storytelling to make your speeches more memorable.

I hope these examples will help you understand that it's your ability to recognize and internalize patterns that leads to mastery. People who excel in a particular field are rarely any smarter than you are. They just spent thousands of hours practicing their craft and creating mental associations. These associations allow them to recognize a multitude of patterns, which is why they can act with what seems like lightning speed.

Now, I'd like you to reflect upon what we just covered and what it means to you. If the world's best grandmasters and Go players aren't actually smarter than us, what does this imply? Doesn't it mean that we have the ability to take our skills to a new level? Doesn't it mean we can forget about our "lack of talent" and start seriously committing to what we want to accomplish in life?

How would it feel to acknowledge that you have the power to achieve your goals if you stick to them long enough? Wouldn't it be much easier to stay patient and persevere?

4

MASTERING YOUR GOAL

66 *One reason so few of us achieve what we truly want is that we never direct our focus; we never concentrate our power. Most people dabble their way through life, never deciding to master anything in particular.*

— Tony Robbins

We've just seen that patience and perseverance are extremely important skills to cultivate. In this section, we're going to have a detailed discussion about another key concept. This concept, which encompasses these two skills and more, is called mastery.

The mastery mindset

Most people fail to achieve their goals because they don't stick with anything long enough to master it. They have the mentality of a dabbler, which compels them to go from practicing one skill to the next. They jump from course to course, program to program, seminar to seminar, and so on. Then, after months of what they mistakenly view as "trying" they have no tangible results to show for themselves.

One of the fundamental problems in today's society is that we have more information at our disposal than we know what to do with. A lot of it is free, which makes it even harder to weed through. It's amazing on one hand, but on the other, it makes it much more challenging to focus on one thing long enough to master it.

To give you an example, I once registered for several free webinars on how to sell more books on Amazon. Next thing I knew, I was bombarded with tons of promotional emails. It was annoying and very distracting due to the sheer volume of content that was being thrown at me. Under these circumstances, it's very easy to get overwhelmed to the point that you don't know what to do next.

The bullet-proof timeframe is one of the tools you can use to avoid this problem. Focusing on one clear goal for the next couple of years makes it easier to stay focused and avoid distractions. However, even with only one goal, you may still have to narrow down your strategies and get clearer on what you should and should not focus on.

The concept of mastery will also help you stick to your goal and get tangible results.

The 5 Commandments of the Mastery Mindset

The mastery mindset can be applied to achieve any goal, regardless of what area of your life it applies to. I hope that you'll adopt the mastery mindset and use it as a lifelong tool to get the results you want.

The key point is focusing on one goal long enough to achieve it and realize how powerful mastery is. Then, you'll be able to replicate the process with any other exciting goals you may have.

Let's take a closer look at the five commandments you need to follow to become a "master".

1. Apply what you learn

Failing to take enough action is one of the most common reasons people don't get results. Rarely do we need to learn more. More often than not, we just need to turn what we already know intellectually into intuitive knowledge. This is done by taking consistent action on everything we learn.

For instance, this book will, in the long run, be extremely valuable to those who take consistent action on it. For someone who reads it and does nothing, however, it's worthless.

In the past, I've had people tell me that my books made a big impact on their lives. On the other hand, I've had people tell me that my books had nothing new to offer or, worse yet, weren't even worth reading. This mentality of looking for something new is what I call the "magic pill" mindset. The question isn't "Does this book have something new to offer?" but rather, "Am I a living proof of everything mentioned in this book? Have I mastered each concept?" That's a much better and more productive attitude to have. That's what mastery is about.

If you were living proof of even a fraction of the concepts you've encountered in books, you'd already be one of the most successful you've ever met.

2. Fall in love with repetition

Repetition is key to success. Behind every success you will find a process of countless repetition. Anyone who has mastered something has done so because of repetition. It's how they mastered their craft. They've been repeating the same actions for years or even decades. It's what you repeat on a daily basis that will turn you into a master. For instance, losing weight is the result of eating healthy food and exercising every day. Writing a book is the result of spending time writing each day. Experiencing more peace of mind is the result of a daily meditation practice. So be sure to make every day count and learn to enjoy to process as you work towards your goal.

3. Focus on one thing at a time

Michael Jordan enjoyed baseball a lot, but he had to make a choice. As we all know, he chose basketball. Billionaire investor Warren Buffet spends most of his day reading. And what do you think he reads about? Investing, of course! He doesn't spend his days reading French literature or science fiction. Michael Jordan and Warren Buffet understand what it takes to become the best in the world. The key point is to focus on one major goal at a time until you get results and trust the process.

4. Master the fundamentals

Are you failing to get results with your goal? Some people believe they've mastered the basics when they haven't, and this common mistake causes many of us to get stuck. It's crucial to get clear on and master the basic skills you need to achieve your goal. Despite the fact that he was already the best golfer in the world, Tiger Woods decided he wanted to improve his game. To this end, he hired a coach, who told him he would have to change his swing. Yes, he had to relearn the fundamentals so that he could improve his game, and he did. Interestingly, his situation is not uncommon. Many world-class athletes go back to basics for the sake of improving their game. That's what enables them to take their craft to the next level. It makes sense, right? Remember, success is the result of a specific process. If you don't get results, there's probably something wrong with the process you're currently following.

If you think you've already mastered the fundamentals, you may want to think twice and go back to basics. Here are two examples of what I mean by that:

- Going through a program one more time to see if there's something you may have missed
- Finding a mentor to help you identify areas in which your fundamentals are weak

5. Think long-term

To master your craft, you need to keep the big picture in mind. You want to have a huge, long-range vision that spans the next ten to twenty years. Your vision is extremely important because it will give you a clear sense of direction. The actions you're taking today will become part of your ambitious vision. As a result, they will carry far more power. Let's say two people are writing a book, and the first person is doing it with the intention of helping a few people. The second person is writing with the intention of inspiring millions of people around the world and becoming a best-selling author. These two people will operate from totally different places. As such, they'll take different actions, which will lead to different results.

Now, for a final reminder regarding the 5 commandments of the Mastery mindset:

1. Apply what you learn
2. Fall in love with repetition
3. Focus on one thing at a time
4. Master the fundamentals
5. Think long-term

Resources vs. resourcefulness

A common trap with goal-setting involves believing that you need more resources. Obviously, having more money or time could make things easier for you. However, these aren't essential to achieving your goal. What matters most is your mindset. You have to develop an exceptional mindset if you want to achieve exceptional results. Money in and of itself can't make up for that. That's why I'm spending so much time on the importance of an extraordinary mindset.

Earlier on, we identified the three most common reasons that people don't achieve your goals. In case you don't remember, the reasons are as follows:

1. Lack of belief in oneself and one's vision
2. Lack of patience
3. Lack of perseverance

These 3 things are all linked to the same thing: a poor mindset. As Tony Robbins rightly says, what you need is more resourcefulness, not more resources.

> *Everything you people have told me. I didn't have the technology, I didn't have the right contacts, I didn't have the time, I didn't have the money. Everything you told me, those are resources. And so you're telling me: "I failed because I didn't have the resources" and I'm here to tell you what you already know: resources are never the problem, it's a lack of resourcefulness. This is why you failed. Because the ultimate resources are emotional states: creativity, decisiveness, passion, honesty, sincerity, love. These are the ultimate human resources, and when you engage these resources you can get any other resources on earth.*

— TONY ROBBINS

Here are some examples resourcefulness:

- Extreme perseverance
- Strong patience
- Unshakeable confidence
- Massive action
- Hard work
- Absolute consistency
- Faith in your ability to learn any skill you need
- An obsession with improvement
- A passion for what you do
- An intense desire to contribute to the world

These are just a few examples, and they're all learnable skills. Would you agree that developing some of these skills would help you achieve your goals?

The bottom line is that you can always improve your skills and create a stronger mindset than the one you currently hold. Don't worry, you don't need to master all these skills in order to achieve your goal. The more you master the better, of course, but just one or two will go a long way.

Imagine yourself having achieved the results you're after. What would your mindset be? What skills must you have mastered to get there?

~

Action step

Use the workbook (section IV. Mastering Your Goal – 1 Adopting the mastery mindset / 2. Resources vs. resourcefulness) to:

- *Rate yourself on a scale of 0 to 10 for each commandment*
- *Write the skills you need to work on to achieve your goals*

~

Adopting deliberate practice

They say that practice makes perfect, but is that really true? In this section, I'd like to talk more about the key tasks that will allow you to achieve your goal. More specifically, I'd like to talk about how to work on them more effectively, which will make your results skyrocket. You can work or practice as hard as you want, but if you do it mechanically without any strategy behind it, you're unlikely to get the results you want.

Practicing piano for thirty years won't automatically turn you into a world-class musician. Writing on a daily basis won't, in itself, turn you into the next Stephen King. Working hard isn't enough by itself. We must first get clear on what hard work is and isn't.

Did you know that doctors with decades of experience don't seem to provide better care to their patients than those with just a few years of experience? That's what researchers at Harvard Medical School found out as they reviewed research on changes in the quality of care provided by doctors over time. You would expect a doctor with decades of experience to be significantly more skilled than one who's just getting started, but that's not the case. The same goes for nurses, and I suspect that it applies to many other professions. Why is that?

Personally, I think it's because the more experienced doctors reach a plateau at some point and day-to-day work doesn't allow them to significantly improve their skills in a way that leads to higher quality care. They may be unaware of the ways they could provide better care. And, in many cases, they don't have access to the right training to help them improve their skills.

In the case of a rare disease, for instance, some doctors might find it challenging to diagnose. A doctor in this scenario would need extremely specific training involving case studies and regular feedback if they want to make continual improvements. Other more passive types of trainings just won't do it. In fact, studies have shown that continuing education in the medical field, such as lectures and seminars, do little to help doctors improve their skills.

I would argue that, in most professions, people reach a plateau at some point. Unless they consciously decide to take their skills to a new level and engage in specific, deliberate practice to help them do so, they won't significantly improve their performance.

What is deliberate practice?

Deliberate practice is what differentiates someone who practices tennis for fifteen years and becomes one of the top players from someone who plays tennis for fifteen years as a hobby. While the first type of person keeps improving their game year after year, the second only improves their game during the first few years of practice before getting stuck in a plateau for years on end.

If you aren't making tangible progress on your current goals, it's probably because you aren't applying deliberate practice. In fact, if you're anything like me, you've probably never used deliberate practice to improve your skills before. This, of course, leaves you with enormous room for improvement.

What exactly is deliberate practice?

In their book *Peak, Secrets from The New Science of Expertise*, Anders Ericsson and Robert Pool define deliberate practice as follows:

- Deliberate practice builds skills for which effective training techniques have already been established.
- Deliberate practice takes place outside of your comfort zone, requires significant effort, and is generally not enjoyable.
- Deliberate practice involves specific, well-defined goals.
- Deliberate practice requires a person's full attention and conscious actions.
- Deliberate practice involves regular feedback that you give appropriate responses to.
- Deliberate practice both creates and relies on effective mental representation (the patterns we mentioned earlier.)
- Deliberate practice almost always involves working on existing skills or building new ones by focusing specifically on some aspect of those skills that need to be improved.

It's not hard to imagine how the use of deliberate practice can lead to better long-term results than simply putting in "hard work". It allows you to work both smarter and harder by consciously focusing on improving the skills you need to reach your goal.

You might be thinking, "If deliberate practice is so great, why aren't more people using it?" There are a few reasons for that.

First of all, deliberate practice must be based on existing training techniques that are effective. It works well with activities for which performance can be assessed like sports, playing instruments, or chess. Yet it's more challenging for other activities where performance is harder to assess, such as teaching or business management.

Secondly, it requires effort. And let's face it, many people aren't willing to go through the hassle.

Thirdly, many people are unaware of deliberate practice and how they can leverage it to improve their skills.

Below are some examples of what deliberate practice is and isn't.

Writing:

Typical practice:

Writing, writing, and more writing. In the words of Stephen King, "If you want to be a writer, you must do two things above all others: read a lot and write a lot." I don't doubt the importance of reading and writing more, but what if it's more complex than that?

Deliberate Practice:

It seems like Benjamin Franklin felt he needed to do more than read and write a lot. He focused on improving specific skills: his writing style, vocabulary, and sense of organization.

- Writing style: He made notes on articles from *Spectator*, a high-quality newspaper, which he would use to rewrite the articles a few days later. He would then compare his version to the original and modify it accordingly.
- Vocabulary: He rewrote *Spectator* essays in verse and then in

prose so that he could compare his vocabulary to that which the original article used.

- Organization: He wrote summaries of every sentence in a particular article on separate sheets of paper. He would then wait a few weeks before challenging himself to write the article in the correct order and compare his work to the original article.

Doesn't that sound like fun? And he did that consistently while holding a full-time job!

Public speaking

Typical practice:

Practicing a certain speech again and again until your performance becomes satisfactory.

Deliberate practice:

Focusing on a specific skill or aspect of your speech that would allow you to improve your overall performance. These skills and aspects include the following:

- The tone of your voice
- Your rhythm
- The structure of your speech
- Your body language/eye contact
- The use of your space
- How you tell stories
- Your vocal projection

Designing your own deliberate practice

The fastest and easiest way to use deliberate practice involves looking at what's already out there. There's no need to reinvent the wheel. How did the best in your field rise to the top? What are they doing on a daily basis? How do they train, how long do they train, and how often do they do it? To make the process easier, you can also hire a coach, find a mentor, or buy programs that address your specific needs. This will help you reduce the learning curve and make faster progress.

There may not be a proven method you can rely on to help you achieve your goals. As such, you may need to create your own deliberate practice.

If so, the process below can be used to do just that.

- Break down the skills you must improve to achieve your goals
- Find out what aspects of each skill must be mastered
- Prioritize them in order of what's most important to master
- Find a way to work on these aspects on a consistent basis (daily is best)
- Find a way to measure your progress

Let me give you a simple example that I came up with.

Example 1: Let's say you're currently studying English and want to improve your listening skills. Now, we need to identify what aspects you need to work on to improve that specific skill

Aspects:

- Vocabulary: Perhaps you're having trouble fully understanding the language because your vocabulary needs growth
- Pronunciation: Maybe you know a lot of words but you can't understand them in conversation because you don't know the correct pronunciation
- Speed: Maybe you feel like people are talking too fast and you don't have time to process their words

Practice:

You could decide to watch a certain movie or video with subtitles until you can understand everything being said without them.

More specifically, you could block out fifteen to thirty minutes of time each day to watch short videos on YouTube regarding a topic that you want to work on. Ideally, you'd start with very short videos (1-2 minutes).

- The first time around, you would listen to the videos and try to understand what is said without looking at the subtitles.
- The second time, you would watch the video while looking at the subtitles.
- The third and fourth times, you would try to understand as much as you can without looking at the subtitles.
- The fifth and sixth times, you would watch the video while looking at the subtitles.
- Finally, you would write down the words you weren't already familiar with or that you couldn't quite catch.

You could also take some notes on how to improve your practice and reflect on any insights you may have. The next day, you would go through your vocabulary list and read it out loud. Then, you would repeat the process we just mentioned.

Once you understand everything, you could play the video at 1.5X or even 2X its original speed and repeat the process mentioned above. You could then repeat the process with more videos around the same topic, regularly going back to the videos you've previously watched to ensure you still understand them.

To measure your progress, you could select a specific video and use it as a benchmark. Ideally, this video would cover a similar topic and you would watch it just once according to a predetermined schedule (once a week or twice a month, for instance). Then, you would evaluate how much you understood compared to the last time you saw it. You could even take it a step further by creating more specific criteria to evaluate yourself on.

That would probably be how Benjamin Franklin would approach it. That's not as much fun as watching an entire movie with subtitles while eating ice-cream, right? No one said the path to mastery was easy!

How could you design a specific training regimen that would allow you to get better results with your goal?

∼

Action step

Use the workbook to write down what kind of practice you're going to adopt to achieve your goals (section IV. – 3. Adopting deliberate practice).

∼

The art of being busy

It's very easy to spend time doing busywork without getting much done. I've certainly done that before. Have you ever spent hours watching educational videos on YouTube while passing it off as work? I've been there. Are you the type of person who reads book after book, believing that you're genuinely making progress towards your goal? I've been there, too.

There's nothing inherently wrong with these activities and they are, to a certain extent, necessary. However, these activities alone won't get you the results you want in life. Most people are guilty of this form of disguised procrastination, because it's easier (and more fun) to passively read books, go to seminars, or watch videos than to take concrete actions. It can also be highly addictive as it gives you the illusion that you're actually working and even learning a great deal in the process. In reality, however, this is often the very thing that prevents you from making real progress on your goal.

If you're reading this book, I can already tell you that you probably

57

don't need more knowledge. What you need is to take more action and turn your current knowledge into experience until it becomes part of who you are. American serial entrepreneur Gary Vaynerchuk is a great example. He confessed that he seldom (if ever) reads books. Guess what he's doing instead: Taking action! Action! Action! Action. The results he gets from that speak for themselves.

We tend to think that knowledge is power, but that isn't true. Knowledge followed by action is power. Knowledge is only potential power. It becomes fire when (and ONLY when) there's a spark. That spark is what we call "ACTION". Without that spark, it remains untapped potential and is pretty much useless.

Now, I'd like you to become more aware of your daily activities and start making a clear distinction between the activities that directly contribute to your goals and the ones that are merely distractions disguised as "work".

Spending hours watching YouTube videos or reading books is a huge trap. Unless, of course, it's followed by tangible actions that move you closer to your goal. I'm harping on this because it's a very common trap that has to be clearly exposed for what it is: *procrastination or addictive behavior in disguise.* If you're serious about achieving your goals and designing the life you want, these activities must be put on the same level as spending hours watching TV, playing video games, or gambling. There's nothing inherently wrong with any of these things. They just aren't work.

Being productive means producing something and having a tangible output to show at the end of the day. It's more than just watching a bunch of videos on YouTube. I can't stress that enough!

Ask yourself the following question: What did I produce today?

∽

Action step

Write down the goal-related activities you did in the last 7 days. Then, on the scale of 0 to 10 rate how each activity contributed to your goal. Finally, write down more effective tasks you could do instead. Fill in the table in the corresponding section of the workbook. (section IV. – 4. Exposing distractions)

~

5

BECOMING OBSESSED WITH YOUR GOAL

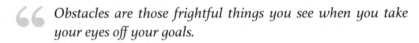

Obstacles are those frightful things you see when you take your eyes off your goals.

— HENRY FORD

How often do you think of your goal? If you aren't thinking of it several times a day, I'd venture to say you aren't nearly as obsessed with it as you should be. In this chapter, I'm going to talk about how you can become more obsessed with your goal and increase your chances of achieving it.

Yet again, repetition is key. To become obsessed with your goals and avoid taking your eyes off of them, it's important to expose yourself to them on a daily basis. You can do this in the following three ways:

1. Reading your goals out loud every single day and/or writing it down
2. Thinking of your goals as often as possible throughout the day
3. Looking at your goals as often as possible by keeping them

on your desk or (better yet!) by keeping them on a wall or vision board.

1. Reading your goal out loud

Once you have a list of goals, you want to read them out loud every morning. This list could be a weekly, monthly, or yearly list of goals.

How to create a list of goals

If you don't yet have a list of goals, I highly encourage you to make one. If you already have a list, I'd like to help you optimize it. I've created some steps to create your list of goals. Refer to the "How to create a list of goals" section in the workbook.

We're only concerned about your ONE goal in this book, so, instead of putting other unrelated goals on your list, you'll write sub-goals and activities. You'll also record any other milestones that must be achieved before you can achieve your ONE goal.

Use the SMART goals methodology

Be sure to use the SMART goals methodology when setting goals. In case you've forgotten, let's talk about what SMART goals are for a moment.

SMART stands for:

- Specific: What exactly do you want? What are you trying to achieve?
- Measurable: Can you easily assess your progress towards your goal? How will you know if you've achieved it?
- Achievable: Is it achievable? Is the timeframe realistic? Can you put in the effort required despite other responsibilities?
- Relevant: Is it in line with your values? Does it excite you?
- Time-bound: Do you have a clear deadline for your goals?

Write your list of goals so that they start with the following phrases:

'I'll easily...', or 'I am'. Using that structure, an example of a SMART goal would be:

- I'll easily publish an amazing book on goal-setting by December 31st, 2017
- I'll easily lose 15 pounds by October 31st, 2017

You can be even more specific. The more specific the better. If, for instance, you're learning Japanese, your goal could be:

- I'll easily have a 15-minute conversation in Japanese with my friend Kei. We'll talk about my travel experiences in Japan (what I did and didn't like and what happened to me) by July 31st 2017

Tips for when you read your list of goals

When you read your list of goals, you don't want to do it mechanically. You want to make sure that these goals are exciting you. To do that, you need to add a strong "why" to each of these goals.

For instance:

- I'll easily publish my book and help thousands of people achieve their most exciting goals and create an extraordinary life.
- I'll easily lose fifteen pounds and feel healthy, energetic, and good about myself.
- I'll easily have an amazing 15-minute conversation in Japanese with my friend Kei and feel proud of myself for speaking so well.

∽

Action step

Create your own list of goals (refer to section V. Becoming Obsessed with Your Goals – 1. Creating a list of goals and to the "How to Create a List of Goals" section at the end of this book)

~

2. Thinking of your goal as often as possible

Can you recite your list of goals from memory? Many people have vague goals. They may take some kind of action towards one of their goals for a short period of time, but after a few weeks or months they completely forget about it. A perfect example of this exists in the infamous New Year's resolutions. People are just too busy. Or they set their eyes on a seemingly more exciting goal, before they even have the chance to get results from their current goal. By going through step 1 (reading your goals out loud every day), you'll never forget about your current goals. They'll remain in the back of your mind constantly and you'll continue thinking of them throughout the day.

Visualization

When you think of your ONE goal, the best thing you can do is visualize yourself as having already achieved it. You want to make it as real as possible. How does it make you feel? What kind of person have you become?

Be careful, of course. You don't want to visualize your goal like the typical person who winds up daydreaming about how they'll successful or achieve X, Y or Z "someday". You want to commit to your goal and vision. You want to reach a point where you feel like you're already there and that there's no way it won't happen.

Another thing you want to do is visualize yourself working on your goal. Studies have shown that people who visualize themselves working on a task are more likely to actually work on it. Whatever tasks you decide to work on today, practice visualizing what it will be like to complete it.

If, for example, my task is to write this book, I can visualize myself turning on my computer in the morning, opening the document, and writing a new section of this book. I can go further by remembering what I've already written and the specific section I'm going to work on today. Finally, I can mentally commit to working on it today. This process takes only a few seconds, but can be very effective in helping you overcome procrastination.

3. Looking at your goal as often as possible

Your subconscious mind is constantly running the show behind the scenes. It's scanning your environment 24/7 and taking in an incredible amount of information. If you want to think of your goal more often, there's nothing better than having it written in a place where you can see it all day long. Read on for some ideas on how you can do that.

- Write your goal on a large piece of paper and put it on your wall
- Have your ONE goal and list of sub-goals on your desk so that you can look at them often
- Create a physical vision board using pictures to represent your goal in a way that resonates with you
- Create a digital vision board on your computer

Focusing on what you want

When thinking of your goal, don't try to move away from something you don't want. Instead, work on moving towards something you do want. It might sound like I'm saying the same thing, but I'm not.

When you try to move away from something you don't want, you're operating from a mindset of scarcity. You're basically telling your subconscious mind that something is lacking in your life. You don't want to focus on your goal from that place of scarcity and fear.

It's easier said than done, of course, and I don't expect you to get rid of your scarcity mindset overnight. However, I'd like you to bring more awareness to your current thoughts to see whether you're acting from a place of excitement and love or from a place of lack and fear.

Personally, I find the desire to make a contribution to the world more effective and inspiring than trying to make money or become famous. Yet I do sometimes find myself in a place of scarcity where I wonder whether I'll make money from my writing. When this happens, I try as hard as I can to refocus on serving people and making a real difference.

Remember that you always attract more of what you choose to focus on. As such, taking time each day to think of what you want and what you're grateful for is a great habit to establish as you work on your goal.

∽

Spend a few minutes to answer the two questions below using your workbook (section V. – 2. Looking at your goal / 3. Thinking of your goal)

- How will you ensure that you look at your goal every day?
  Write down your answer (ex: put it on my desk, on the wall...)
- How will you ensure you spend time thinking of your goal every day? (ex: I will read it out loud, I will write it down. I will spend a few minutes visualize it and how it makes me feel)

∽

6

CREATING DAILY HABITS TO SUPPORT YOUR GOALS

> *Some things you have to do every day. Eating seven apples on Saturday night instead of one a day just isn't going to get the job done.*
>
> — JIM ROHN

So far, we mentioned the importance of setting goals that excite you. We also talked at length about what can be done to create an extraordinary mindset and stay focused on your goals. Now, let's have a closer look at how you can put a structure in place to support your ONE goal.

You are the sum total of what you do and think every day. To make it easier for you to stay consistent and eventually achieve your goal, it's important to implement powerful daily habits that fully support it. Daily habits are great for three reasons:

1. They help develop consistency

Daily habits are fantastic because they help you become more consistent. As we've previously mentioned, consistency is a MUST when it comes to achieving your goal. To assess your consistency of your habits, just look at whether you perform them each day.

2. They help you build and maintain momentum

Working on your goal every day helps build momentum. Once you have that momentum, the last thing you want to do is lose it. For me, slacking off just a little bit can easily make me lose my momentum. I then have to rebuild it, which requires additional effort and energy.

3. They reduce the amount of willpower needed

As you repeat the same tasks every single day, they become habits and require less and less willpower. When that happens, you have more willpower available and can get more done throughout the day.

How to implement powerful daily habits in your life

When it comes to daily habits, there is one golden rule: **consistency over intensity.** To achieve your goal, you need to focus on the process and remain consistent. As a friend of mine says when I lose sight of the big picture: The journey toward your goal is a marathon, not a sprint.

If you start a marathon by running a 100 meter sprint, what do you think your chance of finishing it will be? I've never run a marathon myself, but I would guess that starting it with a sprint would seriously jeopardize my chance of crossing the finishing line. If you have 26 miles to run, why not take your time and see how you feel in the first few miles before even thinking of increasing your speed?

Defining your core tasks

Most goals can be broken into a few vital tasks that, when properly defined and performed every day, will tremendously help when it comes to achieving your goal.

Some examples of core tasks:

- For a writer: writing daily
- For a foreign-language student: studying that language daily
- For someone who wants to lose weight: eating healthy and exercising daily

Once you've identified your core tasks, you'll focus on them every day. Note that the tasks you've identified in the previous section on deliberate practice may, in fact, be your core tasks.

The key is to stay consistent. Starting small is one effective way to do this. Is it better to run 2 minutes a day for the next six months or to run 25 minutes a day only to give up after a few weeks?

Below are 4 keys for the effective formation of daily habits.

1. **Start extremely small.** Ask yourself: Will I be able to do it even when I'm exhausted, extremely busy, or feeling sick? If your answer is "YES", then you've got your new habit.
2. **Do it every day.** Consistency over intensity. It's what you do every day that matters, not what you do here and there.
3. **Do not raise the bar.** If you choose to run two minutes every day, make sure you run at least two minutes. Feel free to run longer, but don't raise the bar to five minutes or ten minutes, for instance. Keep it to two minutes and congratulate yourself for sticking to your habit.
4. **Focus on only one (or, at maximum, two) habits.** Focus on implementing one habit at a time and add one more habit only when the first one is firmly established. Note that it can

take anywhere between three weeks to six months (or even more) to establish a new habit.

Finally, keep in mind that whatever daily habit(s) you choose to implement, the long-term results you'll get from them will yield better results than you currently expect. Simply sticking to a habit every day helps you maintain momentum and allows you to stay on track with your goal over a long period of time.

To give you an example, when John Grisham decided to start writing, he was a lawyer and a new father. He woke early every morning to write his first novel. After three years, he had his first book, *A Time to Kill*, which would eventually end up being a bestseller that allowed him to quit his job and become the success he is today.

What core task will allow you to achieve your goals?

Action step

Define your core task using the workbook (section VI. Creating Daily Habits to Support Your Goals – 1. Defining your core tasks)

If you want a more detailed step-by-step method on how to create powerful habits that really stick, you can check out my book Habits That Stick *by typing "Habits That Stick" in the Amazon search bar or by checking my author page at: http://amazon.com/author/thibautmeurisse*

Creating a morning ritual that support your goals

What's better than starting your day with a morning ritual that will support your goal? A morning ritual comes with some great benefits and can be customized at will to meet your personal needs. Having a morning ritual provides many benefits and will do the following:

- Condition your mind to experience a certain emotion, such as gratitude, confidence, or joy
- Stack your most powerful habits and core tasks to generate exceptional, long-term results
- Help you maintain momentum and build consistency, thereby creating enhanced confidence
- Allow you to work on your mental blocks
- Increase your overall productivity

Conditioning your mind

The results you get in life come largely from the beliefs you hold about yourself and the world around you. Your mind is like a sponge and absorbs everything around you. Why not use that to your advantage by implementing a morning ritual that allows you to condition your mind for success? Let me give you concrete examples from my personal life

Case 1: I was constantly worrying about the future and getting discouraged by the lack of results with my online business. I then realized that the only thing I could do was live one day at a time and focus on what I can do right here, right now. I wasn't going to finish the marathon if I kept mistaking it for a sprint. I decided to redesign my morning ritual to address that challenge. I began spending a few minutes each morning repeating affirmations out loud. "I focus on the process", " I enjoy the process and I make every single day count", "It's what I do every single day that counts", and "If I do what I can today, in one, five or ten years from today I will become the best I can possibly be." I would also put Post-its on my desk with messages like "Make today count!", "Focus on the process", and, "It's what you do every day that counts".

Case 2: I realized that I was constantly trying to escape reality by living in the future. My morning ritual was designed primarily to help me "achieve" my goal, but I was neglecting my well-being and my happiness. As such, I made a decision to redesign my morning ritual to focus on my happiness and emotional well-being. It now includes the following activities:

- Meditating for a longer period of time (fifteen minutes)
- Stretching for ten minutes while listening to gratitude meditations
- Reading a journal in which I write down all the positive comments I've received (book reviews, emails, praises, etc.)
- Adding new entries to the journal whenever I can, which forces me to focus on the positive things in my life
- Repeating affirmations that help me focus to experiencing more happiness

Allow me to elaborate a bit on that last point. As an introvert, it's challenging for me to put myself out there. If I'm not careful, I can easily end up staying home most of time, utterly unable to step out of my comfort zone.

As such, being in a positive mood and feeling happiness is extremely important. It gives me the emotional strength to get out of my comfort zone and record videos, do Facebook Live, or contact people I don't know. To condition myself to experience more happiness, I used affirmations like this:

- I give myself the gift of self-love and self-compassion.
- I allow myself to be happy, fulfilled and content.
- I give myself the permission to experience peak levels of joy and happiness in life, because it gives me the emotional strength and the courage to get out of my comfort zone and make all my goals and dreams a reality.
- When I'm happy, I'm more creative, healthier, and have more courage. My posture is better and my body language is improved. I'm more attractive, confident, decisive, and inspiring.

What about you? What is the one thing you could focus on each morning that would help you develop the mindset needed to achieve your goals?

Below are some of the benefits of having a morning ritual:

1. Stacking powerful habits

Your morning ritual can also be used to stack your most powerful habits that will help you achieve your goal. Once you commit to performing your morning ritual every day, you can include your most powerful habits in it and have confidence that you'll stick to them for the long-haul.

2. Maintaining momentum and building consistency

Have you ever tried to implement a new habit in your life only to fall off track a few weeks later because you slacked off for a day or two? It's a common trap that happens to many of us. It's indeed very easy to lose momentum. Once you do, getting back on track requires extra effort. By having a daily morning ritual, you'll be able to remain consistent and build more momentum day by day, which will significantly increase your chance of achieving your goal.

3. Overcoming your mental blocks

We all have mental blocks that prevent us from reaching our true potential and living the life we truly want. For instance, you may feel like you aren't good enough. You may believe that you aren't smart enough to achieve your goal. Or maybe you believe you aren't confident enough to deliver a speech in front of a large audience. A morning ritual is a great way to work on these limiting beliefs and overcome them little by little.

For more details on limiting beliefs, you can check out my article on the subject by searching for "Step 2: Identify Your Limiting Beliefs – How To Overcome Limiting Beliefs" on my blog.

If you want a more detailed and practical step-by-step action plan to implement a morning ritual, feel free to refer to my book Wake Up Call: How to Take Control of Your Morning and Transform Your Life.

~

Action step

Use the blank space in the corresponding section of the workbook to create your morning ritual (<u>*section VI. – 2. Creating a morning ritual*</u>*)*

~

7

REDESIGNING YOUR ENVIRONMENT

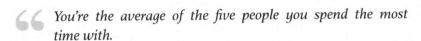

You're the average of the five people you spend the most time with.

— JIM ROHN

Your environment will play a critical role in your ability to achieve your goal. In this section, we'll discuss how you can redesign your environment to help you achieve your goals.

My definition of "environment"

To me, your environment is everything you're exposed to on a regular basis that influences you in some way or another. My definition of the world includes the media (TV, radio, newspapers), the people you spend time with (friends, family, colleagues, etc.), and your physical environment (where you live, the place you work, your desk, and so on).

Why your environment is so important

Your environment influences your beliefs. It impacts how you think, what you focus on, and, in the end, the results you'll get. Negative friends kill your dreams. The media plays on your fears and insecurities while distracting you from what truly matters in life. If you live in a dangerous neighborhood, it will make you feel unsafe and it will probably have many negative role models who lack the mindset you must develop to achieve your goal.

How to deal with negative people in your life

Do you have any negative friends that are suffocating your dreams? They're the ones putting you down and telling you your goals aren't possible. They're the ones telling you to be "realistic" and contaminating you with all kinds of disempowering beliefs. Well, if their view of "being realistic" involves having a mediocre life, do you really want to be realistic? I don't. If you keep spending time with negative people, where do you think you'll be five years from now? Will you be living the life you really want?

Negative people are literally poisonous. Anyone who strives to accomplish a challenging goal needs a supportive environment that will help them get through the failures and disappointments they'll face. They need someone who will tell them to keep going and who will believe in them even when they start doubting themselves. Imagine if your friends were all extremely positive people who were always willing to encourage you. How much easier do you think it would be for you to achieve your goal?

If your so-called friends aren't supporting your decision to take your life in a direction that makes you happy, are they really your friends? Personally, I have little to no tolerance for people who aren't willing to be supportive. I make sure I surround myself with like-minded people who will support me and I avoid negative people like the plague.

If you have negative friends or relatives, here's a 3-part process that can help you get rid of or at least limit the negative influence they have on you:

1. Ask for their support

- Have an honest conversation with them and tell them how you value your friendship and what a difference it would make if they could support you in your new endeavor
- Tell them why you're pursuing your goal and what makes it so important to you
- Explain how their negative remarks, comments, etc. are affecting you and that you can't make it without their support

If they're still not being receptive and are unwilling to give you their blessing, it's time to try a different approach, which brings us to part 2.

2. Limit the time you spend with them

To minimize the negative influence, you must progressively reduce the time you spend with them. Try instead to spend more time with positive friends. If necessary, develop new friendships with people who will be supportive. You may decide to see your negative friends less often. If it becomes apparent that they're not going to change, avoid talking about your goal or anything that could lead to them criticizing or discouraging you. You should also think about whether you want to live your life censoring yourself for people who are supposedly your friends.

If that's something you find unpalatable, or if the two previous approaches don't deliver a satisfactory outcome, you might have to try a more drastic approach. Which leads us to the third option.

3. Cut them off

If these people still have such an impact on your life that is negative enough to prevent you from reaching your goal, you may have no choice but to cut them off. That may be a very hard decision to make, but sometimes it's the right thing to do.

How to design a more inspiring environment

Limiting your exposure to TV and other forms of media

These are also toxic and can be a serious threat to your goal as well. I was shocked to read that, according to a 2016 survey, Americans watch an average of five hours of TV per day five hours per day! This means that, over the course of a lifetime, the average American will have spent fifteen years watching TV! The conclusion I draw from this is that the "I don't have time" excuse isn't an acceptable explanation for not getting things done. Imagine what you could do with an extra 22 years (*if we deduct eight hours of sleep to the fifteen years*). Couldn't you tick off at least a few of the goals on your list with that time?

If you're perfectly content with your life, that's great. If you aren't, you might want to look at how much time you spend watching TV. In doing so, you'll be able to see whether you can use some of that time in a more productive way. That goes for the Internet as well. The Internet is wonderful, but can be a huge waste of time if used improperly.

TV isn't just a time sucker, it's also filling your mind with a lot of crap. It negatively impacts your belief system, destroys your ability to focus, plays on your fears, and tries to sell you things you generally don't need. It makes you think you can lose weight in 30 days without diet or exercise or make money in 30 days just by buying a program. Then, when you fail to get the fantastic results promised, you feel bad about yourself.

You might not be consciously aware of it, but watching or reading the news everyday does have an impact on both your mood and your beliefs. The media wants you to believe that the world is going to hell and distorts reality by handpicking information that suits their agenda. How often have you seen the media reporting joyful events or great news?

Most importantly, watching TV is a passive activity with little, if any, mental, emotional, or physical benefits. Have you ever heard someone say that watching TV helped them create their dream career or achieve the exciting goals on their bucket list? I haven't.

I'd like to go through a quick but enlightening exercise with you right now. Just take a few seconds to recall how many hours you've spent watching TV, movies, or Internet videos the past 7 days. Now, consider the following:

- How much did you get out of it?
- How much of a difference did it make in your life?
- How much has it contributed to your well-being?

Beware, the truth could really piss you off (or set you free)

Fortunately, there are better things you can feed your mind with. You can, for instance, fuel your mind with positive content by reading motivational books or watching uplifting videos. Spending just ten to fifteen minutes reading books each day will allow you to read ten to twenty books a year. As you may have guessed, this is significantly more than what the average American reads each year.

You'll find countless motivational videos on YouTube. Watching motivational videos on a daily basis is a great way to start changing your mindset. I've found Gary Vaynerchuk's videos to be particularly inspiring. He doesn't shy away from pointing out the most common mistakes people make when pursuing their passions. He's also a great example of the mindset you must have to achieve your goals.

∼

Always try to start and finish your day on positive note and stay away from the news and negative television programs as much as you can.

~

Dealing with your neighborhood

It goes without saying that the neighborhood you currently live in also greatly influences your mindset and performance. If you reside in a high-crime area and constantly live in fear, it will obviously be harder for you to create a positive mindset.

If the people you meet on a daily basis are typically uneducated, struggling financially, and hold a victim mentality, it will leave you with very few role models to emulate. If the saying, "You are the average of the five people you spend the most time with" is indeed true, the impact that a negative environment may have on you can't be underestimated.

Yet, in the end, it's your responsibility to design the best environment you possibly can. If you don't do it, nobody else will. It might entail moving to a different a city. Moving isn't cheap, but think about all the things you've been willing to save up for in your life. Chances are, you've put aside money for things that didn't do much for your well-being (a new TV, for instance). A better environment is certainly worth saving for. Creating a better environment could also mean coming up with a plan to spend as much time as possible with people you want to emulate. It might also mean spending your hard earned money on things that will improve your environment.

Redesigning your physical environment to support your goals

Your subconscious mind can take on an incredible amount of information without your awareness. Yale University Psychologists have shown that people who held a warm cup of coffee judged others as more generous and caring than people who held an iced coffee. Similarly, those who had just held something warm were more likely to give something to others. It's amazing how these seemingly simple factors can impact our actions so significantly.

Our minds can be primed in many different ways. If we don't consciously prime them with information that serves our vision and goals, it will be fed with all kinds of negative information.

Affirmations, visualization, gratitude exercises, and so on are all great ways to prime your mind each morning. Carefully designing your physical environment is another great way to prime your mind. Start with the room you spend the most of your time in. If you spend much of your day sitting at our desk, why not design your workstation in a way that supports your goals? Here are some examples of what you can do:

- Put your list of goals on the wall or on your desk
- Create a vision board with all your dreams and goals
- Declutter your desk to enhance your brain's ability to focus
- Put inspiring quotes or words in an area that you can see easily

Optimizing your environment

How much fast food would you eat if it were right next to your desk? How much would you consume if you had to go out to get it? Probably less, right? You want to make your core tasks as easy as possible to perform each day. The less mental and physical effort required, the more likely you are to do it.

For example, if you want to focus on writing every morning, make sure you can easily access the files you need. Removing everything from my desk is something I like to do to make things easier. No cellphone. No food. No documents. Nothing. It's also a great way to condition my mind by sending the message that I'm working now.

Check out some more examples below:

1. If you want to go for a run in the morning, make sure your running gear is easy to get to so you don't waste time looking for them. Not only would that prevent cutting your runs short, it will also help you get going before you have a chance to talk yourself out of running.
2. If you have a creative job, you might want to do what Leo Gura, founder of actualized.org, does. He keeps a pen and paper in every room of his house in case he has a thought or idea he needs to capture.
3. If your tasks involve spending a lot of time on the computer, you want to make sure things go as fast as they can. To this end, your files will need to be well-organized. You also want to create a system that allows you to keep track of information that may be useful in the future.

The bottom line is that designing an effective structure can provide long-term support for your goal. The better you optimize your environment, the easier it is to maintain your daily habits and avoid distractions and procrastination. For these reasons, you should constantly strive to implement things that have the potential to simplify your life, increase your day-to-day focus, and support your goal.

∾

Action step

Spend a few minutes answering the following questions using your workbook (section VII. Redesigning Your Environment):

- How can you spend more time with people that will support your goal? Write one thing you will do. (Ex: I will spend less time with my negative friends.)
- How can you create a more positive environment that will motivate you to work on your goal? Write one thing you will

do. (Ex: I will spend 10 minutes every day writing inspirational materials.)

- How can you optimize your current environment to make it easier for you to work on your goal? Write one thing you will do. (Ex: I will remove everything from my desk when I work to avoid any distraction.)

~

8

REDUCING THE LEARNING CURVE

If you want to be successful, find someone who has achieved the results you want and copy what they do and you'll achieve the same results.

— TONY ROBBINS

Achieving meaningful goals takes time. Yet people largely underestimate what they can accomplish in a couple of years. Regardless of your current situation, you don't need 20 years to change your life. You can start making drastic changes in just a few months, and, if you're committed enough, a few years can be enough to totally transform your life.

To achieve your goal faster, you must realize that your basic assumptions may be wrong. If you currently hold the belief that it will take you fifteen to twenty years to achieve your goal, take a closer look at that belief. Do you really need that much time? Aren't there people out there who achieved similar goals in just a few years? What did they do differently? How can you learn from them?

Yes, you could figure out things from scratch through a tedious and painful process of trial and error. You'd eventually get the results you want, but it would likely take you years. Do you really have time for that? Personally, I don't have fifteen years to figure things out. So, how can we go faster?

Investing in courses

You should always strive to reduce the learning curve as much as possible. Investing in courses, programs, and books is a great way to do this. These are all things that will give you the information you need to achieve your goals. They're great because they offer a clear structure and provide you with lessons to follow. You benefit from the knowledge of someone who has been where you are and knows exactly what needs to be done.

If you choose the right courses, books, or programs (and take consistent action on them) you'll get great results. That's why I like to create a workbook to go along with every book I write. It gives my readers a structure they can follow and increases the likelihood that they'll benefit from my books.

Below are six great tips on how to make the most of the books, courses, or programs you've invested in, including this book. These tips pretty much sum up the mastery mindset that you're now familiar with.

1. **Commit and give it your all.** Once you buy a program, book, or another self-help tool, go all-in. Maintain a mindset that says, "I will squeeze out every ounce of value I can from this! I'll do everything I can to get more than what I invested from it!"
2. **Take action on everything you learn.** Never assume that you already know something unless you've done it repeatedly. Look at it this way: If even one person got great results from the program you're using, you can keep learning until you get similar results.

3. **Master the fundamentals.** In addition to accepting the fact that you probably don't know as much as you think you do, you need to be willing to make tweaks and try new things. Go through the content until you master it, no matter how long it takes. If you don't get the results you expect, just think, "Am I missing something here? Have I *really* tried everything?"

4. **Focus on one book, course, etc. before moving on to another.** Don't be the typical self-help junkie that takes course after course or reads book after book without getting significant results. Focus on one thing at a time and resist the urge to work on every aspect of your life simultaneously.

5. **Be consistent.** Make sure you take some kind of action every single day. When you feel depressed, tired, or discouraged, focus on making minor tweaks to maintain momentum until your motivation comes back.

6. **Be patient.** No matter what you want to change in your life, it's going to take time. Be patient and have faith in the process. Are you trying to make major, long-term changes in your life (like losing weight or starting a business)? If so, give yourself at *least* two to three years to do get it done, and make it your focus on a daily basis. Say no to any new opportunities that aren't in line with your main goal, no matter how exciting they seem. "That sounds interesting! But I'm doing (*insert your goal) right now!" is something you have to get used to saying.

A few questions to help you evaluate programs and decide whether to buy them

- *Do you trust the person who created it?*—Have you followed them for a while and developed trust in them? Do you know people who have benefited from their program?
- *Is this person walking the walk?*—Are they living proof of what they're teaching?
- *How much time and energy will this course or program save you?*

—How much time are you likely to save in the long-run? Consider the cost of the program. If you buy a $200 program and save 100 hours of your time, the program will cost you only $2 per hour. You now have 100 hours you can spend doing something else. This will likely bring you more than $200 if you use this time to work, or $200 dollars' worth of alternative value (emotional, mental, or physical benefits).

* *How much faster can you achieve your goal?*—To what extent will it help you minimize the learning curve and get the results you want? Note that you can easily save months or even years if you invest in the right programs.
* *What is the program or course that, if diligently followed, would allow you to achieve your goal faster?* Remember, there are people who have already achieved what you're trying to do. Make sure you learn from them, as that will yield faster results.

The psychology of expertise

How much time do you think it takes to become an expert? This largely depends on your mindset and the current assumptions you hold.

The Tim Ferris Method

In his popular book *The 4-Hour Workweek* Tim Ferris explains how you can easily become an "expert" in any field. He gave the example of a friend of his who became a top relationship expert in just three weeks. To be perceived as an expert, she did the following:

* Joined trade organizations related to her field that had official sounding names, such as the Association for Conflict Resolution and the International Foundation for Gender Education. This can be done easily online.
* She read the three top-selling books in her field and summarized each on one page.

- She gave one free seminar at a well-known university, using posters to advertise the event. With that experience under her belt, she then gave a seminar at a big corporation.

You can go one step further by offering to write articles for blogs and magazines on topics related to your field.

As you can see, being perceived as an expert may not be as difficult as it seems. Whether or not you're an expert is another story. The point is not to encourage you to become a scam artist. The intention is to show you that you don't need a PhD to put yourself out there and provide people with valuable content. If there's something you're truly passionate about, chances are you probably know more about it than 95 percent of the population. Furthermore, with the amount of information available online and the millions of books you have access to, there's no reason you can't become an expert who provides valuable insights to others.

Whether you want to position yourself as an expert has a lot to do with your mindset and beliefs. If you sincerely believe you can provide value to others and have a compelling vision of becoming an expert, why wait ten years to position yourself as a leading authority in your field? And besides, you want to achieve your goal in your mind long before it happens. You might as well start by thinking of yourself as an expert and conditioning your mind with that belief on a regular basis.

Starting before you're ready

If you really want to reduce the learning curve and achieve your goal faster, there's one fundamental principle you'll have to live by: start before you're ready. In other words, take the leap. Jump forward. Learn to "just do it".

Let's face it, you'll *never* be 100 percent ready. If you wait to be ready, it will significantly reduce the speed at which you can grow and achieve your goal. Or, worse yet, you may never even get started!

Many people believe they have to wait until they're ready to take the next step. That's a huge mistake. Successful people understand that they must continuously move out of their comfort zone to achieve their goals. They learn to be comfortable with discomfort. They just can't afford to wait. As a rule of thumb, the more you move out of your comfort zone, the faster you'll achieve your goals.

Let me give you an example from my own life:

I released my first book in 2015, barely a year after I first began setting written goals for myself. Was I 100 percent ready? No. I certainly wasn't an expert with decades of experience on the topic. I simply kept reading about the topic and learning as much as I could from various experts. Did I provide value to my readers? Yes. I even had one of reader tell me it was as good as books written by some of the experts. Another told me that he loved my book so much that he read it over and over. I'm not saying this to brag (ok, maybe I am), but I'm also saying it to point out that it's better to move forward as fast as you can with what you already know than to wait until you know everything. It's also a bad idea to expect yourself to wake up one day feeling like an expert. It's far more effective to actively work on creating that belief and take action as soon as possible.

Since my first book, I've repeated the process again and again, because I realized that I simply can't afford to wait. I train myself to constantly take action before I'm ready. I wanted to grow faster, so I made a commitment to learn by doing rather than just gathering more knowledge.

You're never going to be ready to do things that truly matter to you. All you can do is get started and be willing to push through the initial discomfort. The principle of commitment, which we'll discuss further in the upcoming section, will help you do that.

~

Action step

Spend a few minutes answering the following questions using your workbook (section VIII. Reducing The Learning Curve – 1. Achieving your goal faster / 2. Failing forward):

1. Achieving your goal faster

- What proven method could you use to help you achieve your goals faster?
- Who already has achieved what you are trying to achieve?
- What bold action could I take to achieve my goals faster?
- What would I do to achieve my goal if I had unlimited confidence in myself?

2. Failing forward

• What could you start doing today to help you with your goals, but don't feel ready to do?

∾

Using commitment and consistency to achieve your goals

Committing builds momentum, which makes it a great way to accelerate your progress. As you commit to something that may be a bit scary, you take one more step toward your goal and the person you want to become. You start burning the bridge behind you, which makes it increasingly difficult to go back to your old self. On the flip side, it becomes easier to get closer to the new you.

Committing to share what I learned by putting content out there as fast as possible motivated me to take more action and become more consistent. After all, putting books out there that show people how to implement new habits and set goals doesn't leave me much room to slack off. It wouldn't be in line with the new identity I created for myself. As such, it became harder to backslide into my old ways.

This book is another great example of how I use commitment to go forward. I want to raise my standards and become one of the top experts in my field so that I can help people make their dreams a reality. Writing an advanced goal-setting book "forces" me to become more committed to my craft and take things to the next level. In a way, this book is as much for you as it is for me.

Taking a step into the unknown can be a little bit scary, but I can guarantee it will allow you get results significantly faster. It will force you to grow and build more momentum as you're working toward your goal.

You'll build confidence as you progress, and will start to genuinely believe you can achieve your goal. This will make you bolder and enable you to take more action.

I don't know what your current goal is, but I encourage you to think about how you can use the principle of commitment to accelerate your results. Whatever you choose to do, it should feel a little bit uncomfortable and require you to get out of your comfort zone.

Start with this question: What am I scared to do despite the fact that it will help me achieve my goal?

Richard Branson, the founder of Virgin, says that "if someone offers you an amazing opportunity and you're not sure you can do it, say yes —then learn how to do it later." I think he summed up this section of the book very well.

A real example of how powerful commitment is

Below is a story from Robert Cialdini's famous book *Influence*. This powerful story how powerful commitment and consistency can be. When used effectively, it can help you tremendously in the pursuit of your goal.

During Korean War, Chinese Communists ran prisoner-of-war camps in an interesting way. They wanted to get some compliance from the American POWs, but, instead of relying on threats and violence, they adopted what they called a "lenient policy". It was, in fact, a sophisticated way to psychologically manipulate POWs.

The idea was to reach agreements on some minor things and to build on that by asking them to commit to seemingly unimportant tasks. A prisoner might be persuade to agree that the United States is not perfect (a pretty reasonable statement considering that nothing and no one is perfect).

Then, he would be asked to explain why by giving some examples. Later, he would be asked to write a list of these imperfections and to sign it. After that, he would be asked to read the list in a discussion group with fellow prisoners.

The Chinese would take it a step further by using what prisoners had written in anti-American radio broadcasts, and naming the authors of each list. With each new commitment, the prisoner would start to change his opinion regarding Communism and begin to believe in what he said and wrote to create a self-image that was consistent with his actions. We, as humans, feel uncomfortable when our actions aren't in line with how we see ourselves. As a result of this "lenient policy", most prisoners wound up cooperating with the Chinese to the extent that few even thought of escape, let alone attempted it.

This story illustrates how powerful committing can be. The more you willingly commit to something, the more you will have to change your self-image to make it consistent with your actions.

Let me give a few more concrete examples of how commitment can be used in the context of setting goals.

Let's say you want to become vegan. One way to do it would be making sure you cook vegan food each day and eat only at vegan restaurants. But how likely are you to maintain long-term consistency?

Here's how you could use the "commitment and consistency" principle of Cialdini's book to maintain a vegan lifestyle:

1. Buy a book on veganism

2. Start blogging about vegan food on a regular basis (writing about why you chose to become vegan, the benefits you're experiencing, etc.)
3. Commit to a challenge of some sort
4. Write an article about the benefits of veganism for a major website
5. Join a vegan group on Meetup or Facebook, for instance
6. Volunteer to help with the group in some way (this might mean cooking vegan food, helping to organize the event, or choosing the venue)

Now, let's say you want to become a coach. In that case, you could do the following:

1. Buy a book on coaching
2. Join a page for coaches on Facebook
3. Write an online article about coaching (you could talk about why coaching is important or how it can change your life)
4. Write a coaching book for beginners
5. Create a coaching blog
6. Position yourself as a coach and offer free coaching sessions

These are some basic examples I came up with. You can come up with many other ideas to leverage the power of consistency and move closer to your goals.

How can you use the power of commitment and consistency as motivation to move toward your goal, speed up your progress, and make it harder to go back to your old self? Write your answer in the workbook.

~

Action step

Use the workbook to create an action plan using the commitment principle (section VII. – 3. Using commitment to achieve your goals)

Write down the commitments you will use to keep moving forward.

~

9

STAYING ON TRACK WITH YOUR GOALS

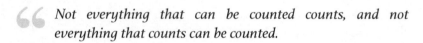

Not everything that can be counted counts, and not everything that counts can be counted.

— ALBERT EINSTEIN

Have you ever set a new goal just to get off track shortly after? We all get distracted in life and, if we aren't careful, it's very easy to get derailed. If something happens that disrupts your routine, such as getting sick or going on vacation, you lose momentum and motivation. Then, next thing you know, you're back to square one. In this section, we'll discuss how to prevent this from happening and ensure you stay on track with your goals.

Creating accountability

Accountability is a necessary component of goal-setting. Who are you accountable to right now? If you don't do what you say you'll do, who will be there to call you out?

I'd like to differentiate between two types of accountability. The first one is what I call internal accountability. The second is external accountability. Let's have a more in-depth look at both.

Internal accountability

Internal accountability is what you rely on to stay accountable to yourself without outside help. It's similar to self-discipline and depends on your ability to follow through on your promises. It determines your ability to stick to a certain diet, go to the gym, or to work on your goals without external pressure. If you lack internal accountability, you'll be unable to achieve your goals without help. You might even struggle despite outside assistance.

The main reason people lack internal accountability is because they keep breaking the promises they make to themselves. As a result, their words have no power anymore. They tell themselves they'll complete a certain task, but they fail to do it again and again. Over time, they totally lose the ability to trust themselves. Once this happens, they stop bothering to set goals or make promises to themselves, because they know they'll just break them anyway.

This becomes apparent in the way they interact with others (and the world in general). They say "Yes" to things despite knowing that they probably won't keep their word. After a while, they're seen as unreliable. When they try to set specific goals, they struggle to achieve them because they have yet to make a habit of keeping their promises to themselves and others.

The more you practice doing what you say you'll do, the more you'll trust yourself.

What can you do to increase your internal accountability?

Tip: Set small goals you can achieve every day to help you build your confidence. See how many days in a row you can achieve these small goals.

External accountability

Many of us lack the self-discipline required to achieve our goals. Yet even the most disciplined among us will benefit from external sources of accountability. If you want to increase accountability in your life, considering the following options:

- Find an accountability partner or become part of a mastermind group
- Join a community of like-minded people
- Hire a coach

Finding an accountability partner

Having someone with whom you can share your goals and be accountable to is extremely helpful.

I have an accountability buddy with whom I share my goals and progress on a weekly basis. We exchange our list of goals every week and discuss what went well, what was challenging, and what can be improved. I've also created additional accountability by sending a schedule to my editor with specific deadlines for my books and articles.

Another way to create accountability is to join a mastermind group where you can share your goals. For optimal effectiveness, make sure that the group's members are committed and willing to call you out.

Joining a community of like-minded people

Being part of community of people who share similar goals will be of tremendous help. You'll be able to ask for assistance, share your goals, and get encouragement. You'll also have an incentive to stay consistent.

I'm part of two groups like this on Facebook, the first of which is a personal development group whose members are committed to changing their lives. The second is an authorpreneur group whose members are a mix of full-time writers and aspiring authors.

I make it a point to contribute regularly and help other people achieve their goals. By doing so, I become more and more committed, which further motivates me to maintain consistency.

Hiring a coach

Hiring a coach is another wonderful way to stay accountable. The coaching process holds many benefits and typically allows you to get faster results. A coach can be expensive, but if you're committed to a specific goal you should be willing to put some money into achieving it.

Additional tips

Tip 1: Telling people what you're going to do

Telling your friends and people you meet what you will do and when makes it easier to stay accountable. Announcing your goals tends to compel you to take action.

You can tell a friend that you'll finish writing an article by Sunday and will send it to them when it's finished. Personally, I like to message my friends on Facebook to let them know I'm going to send them the first draft of my book on a certain day. It helps me push myself and get it done. As I mentioned earlier, I also send my editor a schedule with specific deadlines for the projects I'm working on. I don't have to do that, but it forces me to get the job done.

Tip 2: Changing the words you use

Your words say a lot about your confidence and state of mind. Do you "try", "hope", and "wish" to do things? Do you say "I might"? Or do you say you're "going to" or "will"?

The more you practice using words that show confidence, the more you'll act in accordance with these words. You can start by looking for "maybe", "perhaps", and "I'll try" in the emails you send and practice replacing them with "I will". And remember, the more specific you are, the more likely you'll be to take action. Saying "I will send you my list of goals next Sunday morning" is much better than "I will send you my list of goals".

By practicing the use of confident words, your level of external accountability will increase. That's what I do, and I've noticed a lot of benefits from it. I think you will, too!

$\sim$

Action step

Spend a few minutes answering the question below using the workbook (section IX. Staying On Track With Your Goals – 1. Creating accountability)

How will you create more accountability in your life? (Ex: having an accountability partner, using a specific app, hiring a coach etc.)

$\sim$

Tracking your goals

Without a clear system to measure your results, you can easily get derailed. Evaluating your progress on a regular basis will ensure you're on the right track. I recommend setting aside thirty minutes or so at the end of the week to review the progress you've made. Implementing a weekly review system will do the following:

- **Motivate you to make progress on your goals throughout the week.** Knowing that you have a weekly target and will have to review your progress at the end of the week will motivate you to work on your goals. It works even better if you have an accountability partner to whom you can report your progress.

- **Give you an opportunity to measure your progress and know where you stand with your goals.** By breaking your bigger goals into measurable weekly tasks, you'll be able to better assess your progress and see whether you're on track or need to speed up.
- **Enable you to shed light on potential challenges and things that need improvement.** As you reflect on your progress, you'll identify issues that slow you down. These issues could be procrastination, lack of time, or insufficient motivation, among other things. As you become more aware of your mental blocks, you'll be able to address them properly instead of getting stuck.

How to do a weekly goal review

Your goal is composed of your core tasks and several smaller tasks. During your weekly review, you'll assess how well you performed in regard to these tasks. More specifically, you'll do the following three things:

- Reflect on what went well and congratulate yourself on it (you might even treat yourself with something small if that motivates you to work on your goal)

- Reflect on potential challenges that you encountered during the week— 1) Did you perform your core daily tasks each day? If not, why? 2) Have you completed other tasks on your list? If not, why?

- Think of what you can do to improve next week's results— 1) Did you experience mental blocks that slowed down your progress? 2) Did you procrastinate? 3) Did you get depressed or discouraged? If so, what were the thoughts or triggers that caused those mental states?

Adopting a weekly review system will help you learn more about yourself and your personal challenges. As you become aware of your behavior and thought processes, you'll discover specific patterns that have been holding you back. This process enabled me to identify and overcome several mental blocks, so I highly recommend it!

~

Action step

Spend a few minutes to write down how exactly you will track your goals (IX. - 2. Tracking your goals)

~

10

MASTERING YOUR MOTIVATION

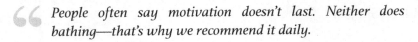 *People often say motivation doesn't last. Neither does bathing—that's why we recommend it daily.*

— ZIG ZIGLAR

It can be challenging to stay motivated. I lost track of how many times I came home after work feeling too tired to work on my online business.

In this section, I'll introduce you to the ways you can motivate yourself when you don't feel like doing anything. After all, the main difference between average people and exceptional ones is that the first group has developed a habit of doing things whether they feel like it or not. Everybody can work on their dreams when they feel excited, but not everyone can work on them when they're not in the mood and would rather watch their favorite television show.

I've identified four emotional states that will help you stay motivated. I rely on them myself. They will all give you the boost you need to go the extra mile. Read on for a list of these emotions.

The four emotional states

1. Love
2. Desire
3. Pain
4. Ego

Love

A sincere desire to contribute to the world and make a difference in people's lives will keep you pumped up as you work toward your goal. When you have a compelling vision inspired by love, you'll be fueled by your vision and the excitement you'll feel about the impact you're making. The more you act from love and the need to give back, the easier it will be for you to stay motivated. This is the deeper "why" behind your goal.

Desire

Desire is different from love in that it's not about contributing to other people. It focuses instead on designing the life you want for yourself. It's about living life on your own terms. Having a goal that excites you will bolster your motivation significantly. Hopefully, your ONE goal excites you. You'll feel connected to your goal, to the point that reminding yourself of what you'll gain from working on it should keep you going.

For instance, my goal is to create an online business I'm passionate about and can make a living from. Here are few benefits I can think of:

- Having the freedom to travel the world while working on my business
- Having the ability to spend time with my family

- Having the freedom to live in different countries and learn foreign languages
- Having the freedom to take vacations whenever I want
- Being able to spend time doing what I love
- Having the potential to earn more money by scaling up my business (which would be impossible if I worked for someone else)
- Being in a situation where I can, and must, grow consistently and become a better person
- Having more time to spend on my personal growth (seminars, meditation, side projects, etc....)

These are all things that motivate me to work on my goals every day.

Pain

Nobody wants to suffer, and we spend a lot of time trying to move away from pain. When used intelligently, pain can be an effective tool to motivate you when you'd rather do nothing. When I was an employee, there were many times when I didn't feel like working on my online business. After a rough workday, I'd go home exhausted and wanting to rest. I bet you can relate to that feeling! I handled it by focusing on the pain I'd endure if I didn't work on my business and create the life I want. I asked myself the following questions:

- Do I really want to work a job I hate for the rest of my life? Do I want to be caught in rush hour every morning for the next forty years? Do I want to have a boss telling me what to do when I already know what I want to do with my life?
- When I reach my deathbed, will I regret not having done what I know I should have? How much pain will I experience when I realize I didn't have the courage, determination, and perseverance to follow my dreams?
- Can I accept the pain and regret of not facing my fear and failing to make a difference through my work?

Usually, the idea of spending forty years at a job I can't stand with someone telling me what to do is enough to give me a serious boost of motivation. Freedom is what I value most, and being unable to enjoy the level of freedom I want is quite painful.

Ego

Ego can also be a powerful motivator. Your desire to be successful, feel loved, or prove those who didn't believe in you wrong, can be used to your advantage.

You might, for instance, feel a surge of motivation when you think of how proud your parents will be. Or the thought of showing someone who doubts you what you're really made of might get you going.

That said, bear in mind that if you feel a constant need to rely on your ego, you might want to spend some time working on yourself. It would be a good idea to figure out why you're trying so hard to get others to validate you.

I've relied, and still rely on, all four types of motivation to ensure I keep going. Read on for some specific examples organized by category.

- Love: Knowing how much of impact I can have on other people's lives makes me excited to work on my books.
- Pain: When I felt tired after work, I visualized myself staying at a job I hate for 40+ years and feeling the pain and regret that goes with it. This gave me an extra boost of motivation that helped me work on my goals for a few hours even when I didn't feel like it.
- Desire: When I feel demotivated, I think of the freedom I'll be able to enjoy once I achieve my goals. This, of course, gets me excited and reenergized.
- Ego: Although I don't like to admit it, I sometimes envision myself having achieved my wildest dreams while others admire the person I've become.

Additional tips on motivation:

If you're still plagued by the urge to procrastinate, try giving yourself permission to work for five minutes and stop if you're still not in the mood. It removes the pressure of having to work for a long period of time and minimizes the fears that come with perfectionism. You'll realize that just getting started is often enough to build momentum and get you "in the mood". That's especially true if your goal is something that you're excited about (as well it should be!).

~

Action step

Spend a few minutes to write down your pain, ego-based and pleasure motivators. (X. Mastering Motivation)

~

CONCLUSION

I'd like to thank you for staying with me till the end and congratulate you on your perseverance. It shows that you're seriously committed to making significant changes and achieving goals that genuinely matter to you.

This book contains a lot of information, and I know you may not be able to apply all of it right away. I'm still learning myself and, as Jim Rohn says, "Listen to me carefully, but don't watch me too closely". You may consciously choose to discard some of the recommendations made in this book, and by all means, feel free to do so. What matters most is figuring out what works for *you*.

However, I do hope you'll come back to this book as often as necessary and review its contents until you become a living proof of its lessons. You've been patient and perseverant enough to read this book, and I'm confident that you will also remain that way while working on your goals. May this book be the beginning of a new and exciting journey for you!

Remember that this journey you've chosen to embark on is a marathon, not a sprint. Not only do you have time, you also have an extraordinary ability to learn and grow beyond your wildest dreams.

You'll face many challenges in the future, as I'm sure you know. You'll feel disappointment, frustration, and fatigue. You'll also find yourself on the verge of giving up many times. It's important to remember that all of this is part of the process. When this happens, reconnect with your passion, focus on your "why", and take another step forward. That's what successful people do.

I'm really looking forward to hearing from you at some point in the future. Hopefully, you'll be well on your way to accomplishing your goal and transforming into the person you've always wanted to become.

As for me, I'll continue working towards my own goals by writing more books and striving to support you and others to the best of my ability.

If you have feedback or questions, or want to share your story with me, feel free to contact me at any time at

thibaut.meurisse@gmail.com.

I'll get back to you as soon as I can.

Don't forget to:

- Check out my blog at: www.whatispersonaldevelopment.org
- Check out my author page at: http://amazon.com/author/thibautmeurisse
- Join my Facebook page at: https://www.facebook.com/whatispersonaldevelopment.org/

I wish you all the best and hope to hear from you very soon!

Warm regards,

Thibaut Meurisse

Founder of Whatispersonaldevelopment.org

GOAL SETTING SKILLS ASSESSMENT - SURVEY EXPLANATIONS

1. Do you have a list of written goals? If yes, how often do you look at it? Y / N

→ The simple fact of writing down your goals help you clarify your goals and make them more tangible. You have now a target you can aim at rather than some vague goals in your mind.

2. How often do you set goals? (Daily/weekly/once a year when you make your new resolutions?)

→ The more often you set goals, the more likely you are to make progress. Indeed, as you set goals regularly, you are forced to chunk down your big goals into small actionable tasks that can be complete in a short period of time.

3. On a scale of 0 (no results) to 10 (great results) how good have you been in the past at generating the results you want?

→ If you have failed to achieve most of your goals in the past, it means that you probably haven't a clear and effecting goal setting method. This book will help you with that.

4. Do you have a clear written plan describing how you will achieve

your goals? Y / N

→ People who have a clear written plan are more likely to achieve their goals which doesn't come as much of a surprise. Having a plan in your mind is not enough.

5. Do you have a system that allows you to remain accountable? (Accountability partner, coach etc.) Y / N

→ With no accountability it is very easy to fall off track (even if you are very disciplined)

6. On a scale of 0 (never) to 10 (multiple times a day) how often do you think of your goals

→ We tend to attract that we think of most of the time. The more time you spend thinking of your goal, the more likely you are to achieve it providing you take the necessary action. Without a proper habit of thinking of your goal on a regular basis, it is very easy to forget about it. Last think you know, this goal you were excited about is gone.

7. On a scale of 0 (never) to 10 (very often), how often do you break your promises to other people? (I.e. saying YES to something knowing you aren't going to do it, or not doing it for whatever reason)

→ If you often break the promises you make to others it means that the words you say have little power. If your words have little power, then how can you trust yourself to achieve your own personal goals, which aren't much different from promises you make to other people. What's the point setting goals if you know you aren't going to do anything about it.

8. On a scale of 0 (never) to 10 (very often), how often do you break your promises to yourself? (promising yourself you'll do something but ending up not doing it)

→ Same as above. If you never do what you say you are going to do, setting goals won't be very effective.

9. Do you visualize your goals regularly? Y / N

→ Visualization can be very effective. It's how many world-class athletes or chessplayer practice. The more you can visualize your goal with clarity and make it as real as possible, the more you start believing that this goal is possible. As your beliefs changes, your behavior and your actions will also change helping you achieve your goals.

10. Do you share your goals with other people? Y / N

→ Sharing your goals is a great way to create accountability. It means that you are willing to put skin in the game by committing to your goal.

However, sharing your goal isn't the same as talking about your goal all the time. A general rule of thumb is that the more we talk the less we do. The more you talk about your goal, the more you feel like you are doing something about it which may prevent you from taking further actions. Be careful!

11. Do you reward yourself for making progress on your goal? Y / N

→ Rewarding yourself is a great way to give you an extra boost of motivation. You don't necessary have to reward yourself when you achieve a goal, you can reward yourself for taking the right action like following through a certain daily habit, or doing something you know you should do even if you didn't get the results expected. Taking what you know is the right action is in itself a positive action that needs to be reinforced. Rewarding yourself for that is a great way to do it.

12. On a scale of 0 (not true at all) to 10 (absolutely true) how true would you say is the following statement: I have a lot of knowledge but I don't apply it as much as I should in my life?

→ One of the main reasons why many people only achieve a fraction of what they are capable of is simply because they aren't taking enough action. For instance, reading 100 books every year doesn't guarantee any result if none of the knowledge contained in these books is followed by tangible actions. You would be far better off taking action all the time without reading any book.

What do you think ?

I want to hear from you! Your thoughts and comments are important to me. If you enjoyed this book or found it useful **I'd be very grateful if you'd post a short review on Amazon.** Your support really does make a difference. I read all the reviews personally so that I can get your feedback and make this book even better.

Thanks again for your support!

Bibliography

Books:

Goals

- *The One Thing, The Surprisingly Simple Truth Behind Extraordinary Results*, Gary Keller
- *Focal Point, A Proven System to Simply Your Life, Double Your Productivity, and Achieve All Your Goals*, Brian Tracy
- *The Magic of Thinking Big*, David Schwartz, PhD
- *Goal Setting: The Ultimate Guide to Achieving Goals That Truly Excite You*, Thibaut Meurisse
- Mastery
- *Peak: Secret from the New Science of Expertise*, Anders Ericsson and Robert Pool
- *Talents is Overrated: What Really Separates World-Class Performers from Everybody Else*, Geoff Colvin
- *Grit: The Power of Passion and Perseverance*, Angela Duckworth

Habits

- *The Compound Effect*, Darren Hardy
- *Mini Habits: Smaller Habits, Bigger Results*, Stephen Guise
- *Habits That Stick: The Ultimate Guide to Building Powerful Habits that Stick Once and for All*, Thibaut Meurisse
- *The Willpower Instinct: How Self-Control Works, Why It Matters, and What You Can Do to Get More of It*, Kelly McGonigal PhD
- *The Miracle Morning: The Not-So-Obvious Secret Guaranteed to Transform Your Life (Before 8AM)*, Hal Elrod

Other

The 4-hour Workweek: Escape 9-5, Live Anywhere, and Join the New Rich, Timothy Ferris

Secrets of the Millionaire Mind: Mastering the Inner Game of Wealth, T. Harv Ecker

Youtube videos:

Type the titles of the following videos in the YouTube search bar

On Patience

- *Overnight Success* (8mn), Gary Vaynerchuk

On the mastery mindset

- *The Mastery Mentality* (7mn), ProjectLifeMastery

On creating daily habits

- *Daily Habits of Successful People: It's All About Routine*, Brian Tracy

On redesigning your environment

- *How Your Environment Affects Your Success* (7mn), Bo Eason

Other books by the author

Goal Setting: The Ultimate Guide to Achieving Life Changing Goals (Free Workbook Included)

Habits That Stick: The Ultimate Guide to Building Habits That Stick Once and For All (Free Workbook Included)

Wake Up Call: How To Take Control Of Your Morning And Transform Your Life (Free Workbook Included)

Productivity Beast: An Unconventional Guide to Getting Things Done (Free Workbook Included)

The Thriving Introvert: Embrace the Gift of Introversion and Live the Life You Were Meant to Live (Free Workbook Included)

About the author

THIBAUT MEURISSE

Thibaut Meurisse is a personal development blogger, author, and founder of whatispersonaldevelopment.org.

He has been featured on major personal development websites such as Lifehack, Goalcast, TinyBuddha, Addicted2Success or MotivationGrid.

Obsessed with self-improvement and fascinated by the power of the brain, his mission is to help people realize their full potential and reach higher levels of fulfillment and consciousness.

In love with foreign languages, he is French, writes in English, and has been living in Japan for the past 7 years.

You can connect with him on his Facebook page:

https://www.facebook.com/whatispersonaldevelopment.org

Learn more about Thibaut at amazon.com/author/thibautmeurisse

WAKE UP CALL - PREVIEW

I. WHY EVERYBODY SHOULD HAVE A MORNING RITUAL

Taking control of your morning

What is the first thing you did this morning? Did you hit the snooze button of your alarm clock? Did you complain about the weather? Did you drink your coffee hoping that it would give you an extra boost to start your day?

Unfortunately, too many people are reactive. By this I mean that they go through life reacting to the things that go on around them often feeling powerless as a result of external circumstances. It is this attitude of powerlessness that starts their morning. They read the newspaper, which tells them how bad the economy is, how violent the world is, and how prevalent terrorism is. They don't choose their attitude, they don't choose their mood, and they don't set clear intentions for the day. They let everything from the people around them to the things they watch on television control them instead.

Regardless of your environment, the reality is that you have an incredible power to create and shape the world around you. This control starts in your mind. It always does. If you aren't priming your mind for positivity each day, you miss out on extraordinary opportunities for growth and self-actualization. In this book, we'll work on creating a morning ritual that creates sincere excitement and will, upon becoming a daily habit, have a major impact in all areas of your life. We'll work together to make sure it fully meets your needs.

Are you living up to your potential?

Most people will never reach even a fraction of their full potential. They'll remain a mere shadow of what they could have been, because they never make the conscious choice to create the life they want. They never sit down to write down what exactly they want in life. They never set clear intentions for their days. As Jim Rohn beautifully said "I find it fascinating that most people plan their vacations with better care than their lives. Perhaps that is because escape is easier than change."

I love this quote. Indeed, we may spend weeks or even months preparing for a vacation, be it within our country or overseas, but how much time are we really taking each year to craft our life plans? I don't know about you, but for most of us, we don't devote that much time to this.

I suspect that this has a lot to with the idea that we don't have the power to transform our lives. Unfortunately, this is a core belief that many of us have. It's something we may have been told by our parents or teachers. Or perhaps society conditioned us to believe that we have to accept things as they are and can't have what we want deep down inside. Most of us are products of our environment. If everybody around us feels powerless during our formative years, we end up feeling the same.

It never ceases to amaze me how powerless many people feel in their lives. I ran into a prime example of this recently when a 26-year-old woman earning an average salary revealed she was convinced that there was no way she could increase her earnings at any point in her life. Needless to say, she didn't believe in personal development.

I was drinking with some of my colleagues a few weeks ago when one of them mentioned that he didn't believe in personal development. That was difficult for me to understand. If you don't believe you have any sort of power to shape your life and go in the direction you want to go, what's the point? If you think it's pointless to improve yourself and condition your mind to adopt new, positive habits, how can you expect to get anywhere in life? A lot of people seem to feel stuck where they are and see no possibilities for a better future. I don't think anyone can be truly happy living with that outlook.

In a similar vein, many people in Japan don't believe that they can become fluent in another language because they "aren't good at foreign languages". As a result, they think I must be some kind of genius to be able to speak Japanese so well. Yet if you consider the fact that I've spent 10,000, if not 20,000 hours studying Japanese and have lived in Japan for many years, my ability to speak the language isn't impressive.

Your daily habits will determine who you become

It's what you do each day that determines your long-term results in life. You are, quite literally, what you do and think on a daily basis. As such, adopting a few simple daily habits can have a profound impact on the amount of success and fulfillment you experience in your life. This is something that we'll continue to see throughout this book. If you look at the people that most of us consider successful, they usually aren't geniuses. They aren't fundamentally different from you. The only difference between you and them is their daily thoughts and actions, or rather their daily habits regarding what they do, what they think, and what they choose to focus on. You can develop these same daily habits to support your personal goals and dreams.

The power of focus

Let me start by asking the following question: What do you think about most of the time? Where is your focus during the day? We have thousands of thoughts every day, but we're largely creatures of habits. Did you know that, for the most part, over 90% of the thoughts you have today are the same as the ones you had yesterday, the day before yesterday, last month, last year, or perhaps even several years ago?

The truth is, everyone has their own set of thought patterns. Yet there's one thing that all of our respective thought patterns share: They lead to a series of similar situations that continually repeat themselves. That's why some people find themselves facing the exact same relationship issues regardless of who their partner is. Do you find yourself attracting the same type of person every time you get into a relationship? If so, you're experiencing another example of the repetitive experiences our thought patterns may cause. Another example of this phenomenon is quitting a job you dislike for a new one you think you'll love, only to realize within a few months that both jobs are more or less the same.

We also go through repetitive phases. We eat healthy for a while, have a binge, return to eating healthy, and then do it all over again in a never-ending cycle. Understanding what you're thinking and why is important. In the last part of the book we'll touch on thought patterns and limiting beliefs. We'll discuss how you can identify them and what you can do to overcome them.

Our brains share the same fundamental characteristics, and they have a fondness for running on autopilot. As a result, it's crucial to make a conscious choice to control your thoughts and focus towards what you want to attract in your life. If you don't, you'll continue having the same unhelpful thoughts you've had for years, will keep falling into the same behavioral patterns, and will never be able to bring about the changes you want most in life.

As self-improvement expert Brian Tracy says, you become what you think about most of the time. He is one of many personal development experts who espouse this belief. If your thoughts control who you'll become and what kind of life you'll have, then learning to focus on what you want to do, be, and experience is one of the most important habits you can develop.

In that regard, my morning ritual has become a very effective way to focus my thoughts, stay on track with my goals, and remind me of my overall vision. I hope yours will allow you to do the same. We'll work together on creating a morning ritual that allows you to focus on what truly matters to you.

How I learned about morning rituals

I first heard about morning rituals from renowned motivational speaker Tony Robbins while watching some of his YouTube videos. These videos sparked my interest in incorporating a morning ritual into my own life. Since then, I got interested in implementing a morning ritual in my life. Despite my interest, however, I continually failed in my attempts to create a morning ritual. I tried Tony's program that was available on YouTube, but gave up after a few weeks. I also tried to wake up at 5 am each day because it was "what successful people do". I failed countless times at that one, too.

I knew that having a daily morning ritual would make a real difference in my life, but I just couldn't make it stick. Looking back, I can think of several reasons why I failed each attempt.

The first reason was a lack of genuine, long-term commitment. I didn't fully commit to creating a morning ritual because I didn't take it seriously enough. For instance, I could have committed to a 30-day challenge, but for some reason I didn't.

The second reason is that my morning ritual was an example of too much, too fast, too soon. In other words, it was overly ambitious. Considering I didn't have any previous experience with morning rituals, devoting an hour a day to it was beyond what I could handle at the time. Added to the fact that I was trying to wake up way earlier than what I was used to, it was a recipe for failure.

The third reason is that I had nobody to support me and to hold me accountable during the process. Interestingly enough, I had a friend at the time who was experimenting with Tony Robbins' "Hour of Power" series, but we just weren't keeping each other accountable. We both had great goals and good intentions, but guess what? He failed, too.

How I successfully created a morning ritual

It wasn't until the summer of 2016 that I finally managed to successfully adopt a daily morning ritual. You might be wondering how I did that considering the plethora of failed attempts behind me. Well, it was simpler than you might think.

Long story short, I invested in a program that focused on morning rituals, then made a firm commitment to stick with it. I ultimately realized that the primary reason I failed in the past was because I wasn't committed enough in the first place. To this end, I discovered that investing money in a program created a sense of dedication and the desire to take on a new habit no matter what.

I assume you want the same kind of push I did, and that this fueled your decision to purchase this book. I'd like to take the time to congratulate you for making that decision. You've taken the first step!

Once I started to think of my morning ritual as something that would benefit me for the rest of my life, great things started to happen. I'm now happy to say that since making that commitment to my morning ritual, I've been sticking to it each and every day, apart from a few exceptions that I'll cover later in the book. Now, it's your turn! Join me and experience the benefits a good morning ritual offers.

Learn more at amazon.com/author/thibautmeurisse

THE ONE GOAL
STEP-BY-STEP WORKBOOK

1. ASSESSING YOUR GOAL-SETTING SKILLS

Before we get started, I would like you to spend a few minutes to answer the following questions. It will give you an idea of how good you are at setting goals.

1. Do you have a list of written goals? If yes, how often do you look at it? Y/N

2. How often do you set goals? (Daily/weekly/once a year when you make your new resolutions?) I set goals daily / weekly / monthly / once a year /

other:

3. On a scale of 0 (no results) to 10 (great results) how good have you been in the past at generating the results you want?

0 _____ 10

4. Do you have a clear written plan describing how you will achieve your goals? Y / N

5. Do you have a system that allows you to remain accountable? (Accountability partner, coach etc.) Y / N

6. On a scale of 0 (never) to 10 (multiple times a day) how often do you think of your goals

0 _____ 10

7. On a scale of 0 (never) to 10 (very often), how often do you break your promises to other people (I.e. saying YES to something knowing you aren't going to do it, or not doing it for whatever reason)

0 _____ 10

8. On a scale of 0 (never) to 10 (very often), how often do you break your promises to yourself (promising yourself you'll do something but ending up not doing it)

0 _____ 10

9. Do you visualize your goals regularly? Y / N

10. Do you share your goals with other people? Y / N

11. Do you reward yourself for making progress on your goal? Y / N

12. On a scale of 0 (not true at all) to 10 (absolutely true) how true would you say is the following statement: I have a lot of knowledge but I don't apply it as much as I should in my life?

0 _____ 10

2. SETTING GENUINELY EXCITING GOALS

1. Getting Cristal Clear

Assuming you could have absolutely anything you want in life, what goals would you set? Write down below

WHAT YOU REALLY WANT.

To help you try answering the following questions first.

1. If all your family and friends were dead (and you had no social pressure) what would you do with your life?
2. What is it that you want but that you've talked yourself out of because it didn't seem "realistic"?
3. What is it that is really exciting you and that you can't wait to make happen in your life?

Now imagine that you could have absolutely anything you want in life? What would that be?

Feel free to jot down any goals or dreams you have on a separate sheet of paper before writing them down below.

What I really want:

2. Selecting your ONE goal

If a genie coming out of a bottle told you that you could achieve one of these goals, but only ONE, in the next 24 hours, which one would that be? Circle it.

Your ONE exciting goal:

3. Chunking down your exciting goal

Now that you've selected your goal, we are going to chunk it down into manageable and specific tasks using the S.M.A.R.T goals methodology

SMART stands for:

- **Specific:** What exactly do you want? What are you trying to achieve?
- **Measurable:** Can you easily assess the progress towards your goal? How will you know if you've achieved it or not?
- **Achievable:** Is it achievable? Is the timeframe realistic? Can you put in the effort required despite other responsibilities?
- **Relevant:** Is it in line with your values? Is it exciting you?
- **Time-bound:** Do you have a clear deadline for your goals?

Write down your yearly, quarterly and monthly goal.

My SMART Yearly goal:

My SMART 90-day goal:

My SMART Monthly goal

4. Clarifying your why

Let's forget about the how for now and focus on your why instead.

Why is that goals important to you? How do you want that goal to make you feel? Write down your answers below

5. Aligning your goal with your core values

What are your core values? (I.e. things that matter the most to you in your life) Ex: integrity, freedom, family, courage, contribution

What emotional benefit are you after? (I.e. how achieving that goal will make you feel?)

Is your goal in line with your core values? In what way is it an expression of who you are/who you want to be?

3. CREATING AN EXTRAORDINARY MINDSET

1. Believing in yourself

Let's be honest. On a scale of 0 to 10, how confident are you that you will achieve the one monthly goal that you just set in the next thirty days?

If your answer is less than 7 or 8 out of 10, you might have to reevaluate your goals. Don't worry. We'll also work on strengthening your belief and your mindset in the coming sections.

Your confidence level:

0   10

2. Creating your goal-related identity

How will you introduce yourself and your exciting goal to someone you've just met?

Write down how you'll introduce yourself and your goals to someone you've just met, if you were absolutely confident in your ability to achieve it. Think of it as an exercise where you want to **make that person believe in your goal.**

Read it and practice is on a regular basis until it becomes part of who you are.

Your goal identity:

3. Aligning yourself with reality and facing the truth

What is one goal that you wanted to achieve in the past but didn't?

According to you, what are the reasons why you failed to achieve that goal?

-

-

-

What could have you done differently to help you achieve that goal?

4. Mastering the art of extreme perseverance

Your worse cases scenarios:

-

-

-

What would make you give up on your goals? Examples:

- If I made absolutely no money after a year working on my online business
- If I didn't sell at least X copies of my book within 6 months

What would make you give up on your goal:

-

-

-

5. Creating a bullet-proof timeline

I declare hereby that: I will keep working on my SMART goal until

_____/_____/20_____

My SMART goal is:

I will master the 5 Commandments of the Mastery Mindset:

1. Applying what I learn
2. Falling in love with repetition
3. Focusing on one thing at a time
4. Mastering the fundamentals
5. Having the long-term in mind

Concretely:

- I will avoid:

- Pursuing a different opportunity that sounds more attractive
- Giving up when I don't get the results I want short-term

- I will remind myself:

- That I have time
- That I must take action on what I learn
- That it is what I do every day that truly matters not the short-term results

Your name:

Today's date:

Your accountability partner name:

6. Focusing on the process

Now, let's turn your result-oriented goal into process-oriented goal. Write down your current goal and your process-oriented goal you will work on to achieve that goal.

Your current goal:

Your process-oriented goal:

4. MASTERING YOUR GOAL

1. Adopting the mastery mindset

As a means to bring awareness on your current mindset, rate yourself on a scale of 0 to 10 for each of the following

Applying what I learn:

0 _____ 10

Falling in love with repetition:

0 _____ 10

Focusing on one thing at a time:

0 _____ 10

Mastering the fundamentals:

0 _____ 10

Having the long-term in mind:

0 _____ 10

2. Resources vs. resourcefulness

What skills that, if you could further develop, would help you the most with your goals? Ex: self-discipline, perseverance, self-esteem, communication skills...

-

-

-

3. Adopting deliberate practice

What kind of deliberate practice will you adopt to help you achieve your exciting goal? Skills you want to develop:

-

-

-

Specific aspects you need to work on:

-

-

-

Practice you will adopt:

-

-

-

4. Exposing your distractions

Fill in the table below with the goal-related activities you did in the last seven days. Be honest with yourself. On the scale of 0 to 10 rate how each activity contributed to your goal. Then, write down in the right column whether you could have spend your time on more effective tasks instead.

My goal-related activities	Effectiveness (0 to 10)	More effective tasks

5. BECOMING OBSESSED WITH YOUR GOAL

1. Creating a list of goals

Create a list of goals using the related worksheet "How to create a list of goals" at the end of this workbook

2. Looking at your goals as often as possible

How will you ensure that you look at your goal every day? Write down your answer below (ex: put it on my desk, on the wall...)

3. Thinking of your goal as often as possible

How will you ensure you spend time thinking of your goal every day? Ex: I will read it out loud, I will write it down. I will spend a few minutes visualize it and how it makes me feel.

6. CREATING DAILY HABITS TO SUPPORT YOUR GOALS

1. Defining your core daily task

Write down your core daily tasks that will help you achieve your goal (up to three). The following questions will help you identify your core tasks: if you focus on these core tasks every single day will you achieve your goal? Your core task can also be the deliberate practice you previously came up with

Your core task(s):

-

-

-

2. Creating a morning ritual

Use the space below to create your own morning ritual

7. REDESIGNING YOUR ENVIRONMENT

How can you spend more time with people that will support your goal? Write one thing you will do. (*Ex: I will spend less time with my negative friends.*)

How can you create a more positive environment that will motivate you to work on your goal? Write one thing you will do. (*Ex: I will spend 10 minutes every day writing inspirational materials.*)

How can you optimize your current environment to make it easier for you to work on your goal? Write one thing you will do. (*Ex: I will remove everything from my desk when I work to avoid any distraction.*)

8. REDUCING THE LEARNING CURVE

1. Achieving your goal faster

Use the free space below or a separate piece of paper and write down all the things you could do to achieve your goal faster. Below are a few questions to guide you:

- What proven method could you use to help you achieve your goals faster?
- Who already has achieved what you are trying to achieve?
- What bold action could I take to achieve my goals faster?
- What would I do to achieve my goal if I had unlimited confidence in myself?

2. Failing forward

What you could do start doing today to help you with your goals, but that you don't feel ready to do?

3. Using commitment to build momentum

Now, based on the answers you gave in the previous section "failing forward" let's create together a plan that will move you forward using the principle of commitment and consistency. What commitments will you use to keep moving forward?

Your plan of action:

9. STAYING ON TRACK WITH YOUR GOALS

1. Creating accountability

How will you create more accountability in your life? Ex: having an accountability partner, using a specific app, hiring a coach etc.

Your accountability method:

Refer to the accountability checklist to help you make the most out of your accountability partner

2. Tracking your goals

It is important to keep track of your progress as you are working towards your goals. You may want to review your progress at the end of every week or twice a month. It is up to you to experiment with different systems and to design a tracking system that works for you.

Write down below how exactly you will track your goals:

10. MASTERING YOUR MOTIVATION

How will you use your emotions to motivate you to keep working on your goal?

Pain

What will be the most painful consequences of not achieving your goals? Ex: living a life or regret, the pain of knowing what I can do better with my life, the pain of disappointing my love ones.

Your pain motivator(s):

-

-

-

Ego

How can you use your ego to feel motivated to work on your goals? Ex: I want to prove that person wrong, I want my parents to be proud of me, I want people to see how great I am

Your ego-based motivator(s):

-

-

-

Momentum

What will you do to just get started on a task when you don't feel like it? (Ex: sit on my desk, open the word file and start typing for five minutes)

Additional tip: visualize yourself working on the task and completing it and imagine how it would make you feel

Pleasure

What are the most exciting benefits that your goal will provide you? Ex: I will make a living doing what I love, I'll have more free time to spend with my family, I will feel more confident and proud of myself

Pleasure motivator(s):

-

-

-

How to Create a List of Goals

1. Use the SMART goals methodology

Whenever you set goals you want to make sure that you use the SMART goals methodology. Let me remind it to you: SMART stands for:

- Specific: What exactly do you want? What are you trying to achieve?
- Measurable: Can you easily assess the progress towards your goal? How will you know if you've achieved it or not?
- Achievable: Is it achievable? Is the timeframe realistic? Can you put in the effort required despite other responsibilities?
- Relevant: Is it in line with your values? Is it exciting you?
- Time-bound: Do you have a clear deadline for your goals?

2. Write your list of goals using the following format: I'll easily.... Or I am

Now that you have your list of goals you can write each one of your goals using either "I'll easily" or the present tense "I + verb ". An example of a SMART goal using that formula would be:

- I'll easily publish an amazing book on goal setting by December 31st 2017
- I'll easily lose 15 pounds by October 31st 2017 You can even be more specific. The more specific the better.

If you are learning Japanese for instance your goal could be:

- I'll easily have a 15 minutes conversation in Japanese with my friend Kei talking about my traveling experiences in Japan

(what I liked/didn't liked, episodes that happened to me etc.)
by July 31st 2017

Additional tip when you read your list of goals: When you read out your list of goals you don't want to read it mechanically, you want to make sure that these goals are exciting you. In order to do that, you want to add a strong why to each of these goals

For instance:

- I'll will easily publish my book on goal setting and help thousands of people all around the world to achieve their most exciting goals and create an extraordinary life
- I'll easily lose fifteen pounds feeling incredibly healthy, full of vitality and feeling great about myself
- I'll easily have an amazing fifteen minutes conversation in Japanese with my friend Kei while feeling proud of myself for speaking Japanese so well

Accountability Partner Checklist

To ensure that you stay on track with your goals I encourage you to work together with an accountability partner. Below is a guideline you can use when you contact your accountability partner.

Contact your accountability partner and tell him or her:

- What your SMART goals exactly is

- What exactly do you want to accomplish exactly and by when? What is your bullet proof-timeline?

- What you commit to

- What exactly do you commit to do? Will you send your accountability partner a list of goals every week? Every month? Clary state orally what you commit to do.

- Why it matters to you

- What is your why? What will be the consequences if you don't achieve that goal?

- How you'll communicate your progress

- Will you be using emails, phone calls, real meeting?
- How often will you communicate your progress?

- What will happen if you succeed/fail

- What will be the reward?
- What will be the punishment? - Will you give money to your partner or will you give money to an associating going against your value etc.

Additional tip: send your monthly, quarterly and yearly SMART goals (along with your ultimate goal) to your accountability partner.

Key point: Make sure that you are as specific as possible and that your partner is someone who understands the importance of your goal and takes it seriously. The more disciplined your partner is the better.